THE FUTURE OF JESUS

DOES HE HAVE A PLACE IN OUR WORLD?

PETER JENSEN

 matthiasmedia

The Future of Jesus
2nd edition
© Matthias Media 2008

Originally published by ABC Books for the Australian Broadcasting Corporation.
First published December 2005.

Matthias Media
(St Matthias Press Ltd ACN 067 558 365)
PO Box 225
Kingsford NSW 2032
Australia
Telephone: (02) 9663 1478; international: +61-2-9663-1478
Facsimile: (02) 9663 3265; international: +61-2-9663-3265
Email: info@matthiasmedia.com.au
Internet: www.matthiasmedia.com.au

Matthias Media (USA)
Telephone: 724 964 8152; international: +1-724-964-8152
Facsimile: 724 964 8166; international: +1-724-964-8166
Email: sales@matthiasmedia.com
Internet: www.matthiasmedia.com

ISBN 978 1 921441 07 3

Cover design and typesetting by Lankshear Design Pty Ltd.

About this new edition

The Future of Jesus was originally delivered as the 2005 Boyer Lectures, an annual series of radio talks presented by the Australian Broadcasting Corporation (ABC), and published by ABC Books. This new edition contains minor updates and adaptations, particularly in view of a broader readership beyond Australia.

For Beth and Anna

Contents

Acknowledgements

Many people offered me advice and expertise in helping to prepare the lectures that have become this book. I am most grateful to the then Chairman of the ABC, Mr Donald McDonald, for his kind invitation to deliver the lectures in 2005. Likewise, members of the ABC staff have been most helpful, particularly Janne Ryan as producer, Jenny Parsonage, sound engineer, and Susan Morris-Yates, who edited the first edition of *The Future of Jesus*. I am also grateful to Tony Payne and Matthias Media for publishing this second edition.

In their own special way each of the following also made their contribution—Paul Barnett, Paul and Heather House, Bruce Langtry, David Dockrill, Armon Hicks, Karin Sowada, Stuart Piggin, James Haire, Edwin Judge, Dani Scarratt, Michael Jensen, Robert Linders, Keith Mascord, Ann Macklin, Phillip Jensen, Bill Hurditch, Robyn Powell, Keith Mason, Christine Jensen, John Utting and Jenny Price. I thank them all.

1 | Jesus and his future

I've spent most of my life talking to people about Jesus, my great enthusiasm. But it's a job that's getting harder. I wonder how the future of Jesus and the future of our civilization will intersect. Let me illustrate from what I see happening in my own patch of the Western world—in Australia.

Four of our brightest and best—university medallists, historians, lawyers, Harvard graduates, first-class honours men—have written a book called *Imagining Australia: Ideas for our Future*. It is a work of bold and imaginative suggestions.

Rightly, they put a discussion of Australian values in the first chapter, headed 'Australian National Identity'. After all, it's hard to imagine the future without starting with matters of beliefs, identity, ethics, relationships, history.

But they do not have much room for Jesus in their vision of our future. They see that we need values, but they favour humanist values. They seem to think that a secular state means a secular community. Perhaps they think that multiculturalism has disaffiliated Jesus; he is too divisive to be allowed to speak.

I wonder, though, how much they actually know about Jesus. It may be that they lack the requisite knowledge to bring him into the discussion. As an authority they casually quote, for example, Abraham Lincoln saying, "a house divided against itself cannot stand".[1] No doubt he did say this. But Lincoln knew quite well, as did all his hearers, that he was quoting Jesus. He was citing a supreme cultural authority so he did not have to offer a footnote.

So it appears we have now reached a stage where four highly educated and intelligent Australians apparently fail to recognize a standard quote from the Bible. It explains, I suppose, the absence of Jesus from their treatment of values.

Mind you, it is a surface absence because, whether they know it or not, Jesus is basic to our history and therefore to our culture. Thus, when they are trying to upgrade traditional Australian characteristics such as a 'fair go', Jesus pops up anonymously. In a truly striking sentence they say: "The modern fair go demands that we should do unto others as we would have done unto ourselves".[2]

Here again there is the utterly unconscious quoting of Jesus as a source of modern secular values. And there is the lovely irony that the modern fair go is described in the antique English of "do unto others"—straight out of the King James version of Jesus' Sermon on the Mount.

Jesus is there but he's been rendered invisible. He is an anonymous Jesus; he makes his contribution without acknowledgement. And that's one of the main challenges of the job I am doing.

Frankly, Jesus is slipping out of memory and imagination. We cannot really blame the authors of the book. As historian Stuart Piggin has observed, "Australia's social commentators and historians are tone deaf to religion".[3] Dr Piggin documents the way in which the cliché that this is a country without a religious past is religiously repeated.

Professor Brian Dickey of Flinders University is just as trenchant:

> The secular left liberal accounts of our history which became so dominant from 1950 to 1980 did not want to treat with Christianity, except to scorn it ...[4]

What is true in Australia, is also true in different ways across the Western world. In the modern secularized West, Jesus' kingdom has waned, you could say. His future is very unsure. And we have other gurus now. People seem to know so little about Jesus that they are unwilling or unable to refer to him explicitly in a discussion of values. We cannot bring him to the table to tell us what he thinks.

But—and here is a paradox indeed—another reason for his invisibility is that he is very well known. He is like the life of the party—everybody knows Jesus. His kingdom continues to wax, you could say. In fact, he is so well known, we do not even have to think or talk about him. Which means, I submit, that we apprehend him via cultural clichés that hide the real Jesus from view. We do not know him all that well. Parts of his basic teaching would surprise us.

This leads me to another problem: it's the churches who talk mainly about Jesus, and who wants to hear what they have to say? This is a significant problem for me in writing this book. I am, after all, a denominational official —an archbishop no less. I carry the burden of the uncertain reputation of the churches. It is difficult to get beyond the boredom, indifference or antagonism that many people feel towards organized religion.

Perhaps it would be better for me to stick to something safe, like botany or golf, or even values or social justice.

Why Jesus?

For three main reasons.

First, because it is simply a fact that he is one of the two or three most influential people who have ever lived. "The name of Jesus", said the American sage Ralph Waldo Emerson, "is not so much written as ploughed into the history of the world …"[5] Most people who have thought deeply about the subject will recognize the justice of this assessment.

Or take these words attributed to Napoleon Bonaparte:

I know men and I tell you that Jesus Christ is no mere man. Between him and every other person in the world there is no possible term of comparison. Alexander, Caesar, Charlemagne and I founded Empires. But on what did we rest the creations of our genius? Upon force.

Jesus Christ founded his empire upon love, and to this hour millions of people would die for him.[6]

Second, his life and teaching have been so fundamentally important to our own culture. I would say that we are actually secular in a Christian sort of way. Many of us, for example, can quote the Sermon on the Mount as a part of modern humanistic ethics without knowing it.

People will always have trouble in understanding Western literature and history, and therefore Western identity, if they know little about Jesus; they will also have trouble understanding the modern world, a world in which the words of Jesus are taken with utmost seriousness, and acted upon, by millions of people, whether in the newly developing China or in the USA. His words have that sort of contemporary significance.

Third, because I think that, as well known as he is, he is still unknown. You could say that his sheer greatness has obscured the facts about him. Before he slips from view we at least ought to ask whether he has some vital and permanent truths to share with us.

I don't really want to talk about the institutional church or even religion. Such things are of marginal interest to me. Even though I quite like going to church, I find it hard to like the institutional organization. And I don't really think of myself as a religious person.

What I really want to do—and what I think each of us needs to do while we still have the chance—is to talk about Jesus, and to let Jesus talk back to us.

Where I live, there is no established church or religion. That is good law; we are fortunate not to have been afflicted with a state church. I also know that we have embraced multiculturalism, and the new and different Australia that is emerging as a result of our immigration policies is a wonderful place. But some seem to think that it means that we now have no basis for our civilization, apart from a few scaled-down general values like a 'fair go' and mateship, the myth of Anzac and the myth of Eureka.[7]

At a time when other cultures seem menacingly assured and powerful, we seem to have become very modest about our own past, very nervous about identifying who we are, very shy of receiving inspiration from some of the greatest words ever spoken.

We keep thinking that our inherent tolerance and decency will preserve us. We are, after all, a liberal society, interested in the rights of the individual, freedom of opportunity, and justice for all. I would suggest, however, that these traits are far more tenuous in us than we like to think. Put to the test, we may well fail them.

When we are no longer prosperous, when we have to struggle for existence, if terrorism becomes a part of life, what would make us stick to these values? Where would we look for inspiration?

If I wonder aloud about the future of Jesus, it is not because Christianity itself is dying. In many parts of the world faith in Jesus is growing at an astonishing rate. But in much of the West, we must now ask: Does Jesus Christ have a future? Is he going to continue to influence us at all? Are we going to keep appealing to him for guidance? Is he going to continue to influence our lives for good? Can Jesus be brought into the conversation about the future? Many of our forebears looked to him as their inspiration when they laid the foundations of Western society. He did not seem to be a foreigner then.

My chief aim in this book is to inspire a widespread, adult reading of the New Testament Gospels. And I want you to understand some of the issues at stake as we read these documents. I want you to see what a surprising man Jesus was; I want to trace something of his impact on the world; I want to see whether there is a trajectory which suggests that there is more to come; and I want to see whether Jesus can speak with something like his old power about central cultural issues such as personal freedom, human relationships and the future of our world.

I was discussing this project with a sympathetic agnostic and she said this: "How can Jesus enrich the lives of unbelievers?" This is a question I would particularly like to address. I am trying to stand where you may be, willing to think as an adult about Jesus Christ but no surer than that. I certainly do not think that I own Jesus in some way. He speaks to us all.

I aim to be like a committed but sympathetic art critic, someone who stands with you before a portrait, who helps you to see for yourself what your own eyes are observing.

The critic cannot take your place. You will have your own perspective, your own angle of vision, your own presuppositions.

While I cannot predict the results, I do know that this discussion is vital, never more so than now. The quest for the truth about Jesus and his future has ramifications that are social political, cultural and personal.

For your part, you may be repelled, attracted, or left indifferent by such an investigation; in the end, you may share the perspective of that famous Beatle, John Lennon, who notably said:

> Christianity will go. It will vanish and shrink. I needn't argue with that; I'm right and will be proved right. We're more popular than Jesus now; I don't know which will go first—rock 'n' roll or Christianity.[8]

Alternatively, however, you may stand with the great French philosopher and mathematician Pascal and say, "Jesus is the centre of all, the object of all; whoever knows not him, knows nothing aright, either of the world or of himself ... In him is all our happiness, our virtue, our life, our light, our hope."[9]

What do we make of Jesus? Why do I say that we hardly know one of the most famous, the most universal of all men? As usual, there is a history behind these questions.

Almost for the first time, between the 17th and the 19th

centuries many intellectuals expressed an 'enlightened' attitude to Jesus. This enlightenment meant that people began to study the so-called 'Jesus of history' rather than the Christ of the Gospels—biography rather than theology; and miracles became as implausible as the tooth fairy.

The Church worshipped Jesus as both God and man, but the new rationalism accepted his humanity while rejecting his divinity. This new attitude became widespread in the community and that created a problem. What do you *do* with Jesus? How do you explain his sheer historical importance while denying his divinity?

The favourite answer was to turn him into the supreme moralist, to say that he taught us how human life is to be lived. He became a sort of peasant ethicist, a Galilean Socrates, a model human, a religious genius. In the reverent, but irreverent, words of Thomas Carlyle, the 19th-century thinker and historian, he was "the greatest of all Heroes".[10]

The difficulty of this is with Jesus himself, because he is an awkward person to categorize. It's hard to know why the Jesus of the 'enlightened' was crucified. Of course his teaching has moral implications, but he is not like a moral tutor, not like a philosopher, not like a hero, not like a pedagogue.

He was actually more like a man carrying a sandwich board proclaiming the end of the world. He was a man of the future. And that's why he is unknown. If you asked for a popular summary of the teaching of Jesus, then "Love one another" would almost certainly be the reply. Perhaps, to bring it right up to date, the reply would be: "Include one another and don't discriminate; give everyone a fair go and be good mates". But if you had asked Jesus to summarize his teaching, he would have said: "God's kingdom is near; get ready for it".

This is the conundrum: Jesus is universal, so he must have said really important things; but the things he did say are so particular, so time-bound, that they are not important—unless he is divine. So who is Jesus?

To answer this let's start with the basics. Let's start with what he said, and how the information has reached us.

The New Testament contains four Gospels—Matthew, Mark, Luke and John—written in the quite common Greek of the day. Matthew's Gospel has him beginning his public life with this message: "Repent, for the kingdom of heaven is at hand" (4:17).

Mark, probably the earliest of the Gospels, has him saying this: "The time is fulfilled, and the kingdom of God is at hand; repent and believe in the gospel" (1:15). Both Gospels clearly regard this announcement as the burden of his message, the theme and the substance of the Gospels.

But, if so, why can't they agree? Why does Matthew report his words as "kingdom of heaven" and Mark, "kingdom of God"? To answer that, we need to take a brief detour, which will help us see how the information about Jesus has reached us. The puzzle in this case is a relatively easy one to resolve. Matthew is reflecting, or perhaps respecting, Jewish scruples about naming God aloud; 'heaven' is a euphemism for 'God'. On the other hand, Mark, writing, as it is believed, to a non-Jewish audience, speaks directly of 'God' and 'the kingdom of God'.

But what did Jesus himself say? Strictly, neither; he probably spoke Aramaic rather than Greek.

Our knowledge of Jesus is mediated by the Gospel writers in all sorts of ways. The perspective of the writers is one of the things that needs to be allowed for in any assessment of Jesus. The writers have already translated him linguistically. Their special interests will also 'translate' him historically. If we cannot accept this mediated, translated Jesus, we will have to find some other Jesus, for that is how the Gospels are.

To return to the task of getting to grips with the main theme of Jesus' teaching: it is clear from Mark and Matthew that he placed special emphasis on saying "the kingdom of God is at hand". When he said things such as "turn the other cheek", "love one another" or "blessed are the poor in spirit", it was because the kingdom of God was near. His call for righteous behaviour had a huge, hurrying urgency about it.

And what is this kingdom? In that time and place it was a very tricky phrase, stirring powerful emotions. Hundreds of years before, the people of Israel had enjoyed a successful period of history as a rich and powerful empire under the reign of David, who, in turn, saw himself to be under the reign, or kingdom, of God. In a way the kingdom of God had come with David.

But that was far in the past. Closer to the time of Jesus, the recent history of Israel had been one of foreign domination and exploitation—by the Assyrians, Babylonians, Greeks, and then by the Romans. David's former kingdom was now merely an out-of-the-way province of that powerful empire.

As usual under such circumstances, there were different ways of reacting to foreign rule. Think of occupied Europe during World War II: some collaborated, some conformed, some conspired, some revolted, but most at least hoped. I guess that in World War II the hope of the enslaved people lay in Allied power. Some certainly believed in a Providence that would bring peace, freedom and justice. But they had no promise of this, no certainty.

Those who heard Jesus preach reacted to Roman rule in similar ways. Some, for example, collaborated. The difference was, however, that they had a history of a promise-keeping God. God had freed them from Egypt, as he said he would; God had freed them from exile in Babylon, as he said he would; God would do it again, because he said he would.

They were able to contrast their present miserable situation, as a nation under bondage to Rome and her lackeys, with the glowing promises of God for a national, indeed a universal, renewal. To them, God had a proven track record as a keeper of promises.

Why were the Israelites under the heel of Rome? They

did not read this situation as mere power politics; they read it in moral and spiritual terms. They understood that it had something to do with their own evil and with God's justice. And they hoped that God would save them. As a result, they were waiting for an open manifestation of the kingdom of God. The kingdom would include the putting to rights of all things, the judgement on the wicked inside and outside their own community, and the elevation of the righteous. It would usher in a new heaven and a new earth. This belief gave their national life a depth that is hard for us to imagine, let alone experience.

By now it will be obvious that two major factors shaped the original listeners. The first was their scriptures. They belonged to a nation of the Book; they lived in a world in which the teachings of the Book were the staple intellectual and spiritual diet. It provided them with their framework of meaning.

It's hard for us to understand this, because we have lost the sense of identity that a shared history created. In our national life there is now a vacuum where most people have a history. It's hard to find meaning, purpose and community without it.

The four authors of *Imagining Australia* know this. It is why they suggest that we begin to make the story of Eureka—the 1854 uprising by diggers in the goldfields of Victoria—our national myth. To me, Eureka seems rather weak on capacity to inspire and shape; even the authors admit that the story has never before "been so marginal and unimportant for most Australians" as it is now.[11] How it will sustain humanistic Australian values in the hard years that may well lie ahead is impossible to imagine.

Even appropriating the biblical history of Israel as if it were our own could be a better option. It has certainly been done before now; think of how the biblical story sustained the American slaves.

The Bible was the history book of the Jewish nation at the time of Jesus. But it was more than mere antiquity: it was filled with a powerful sense of promise, of time waiting to be fulfilled, of events still to come. It was promise on one side, and faith on the other. In the end it became the history book of and for Western culture, not just the slaves. It provided for us, until very recent times, the dynamic of hope in a world without clear meaning, purpose or community. We have lost the biblical narrative, but we have not replaced it.

There were two key factors shaping the original hearers of Jesus' words: the first was the Bible, and the second was their political situation. Here, all their hopes collided with all their fears. In this climate, one option was violent terrorism and insurrection. According to ancient historian Paul Barnett: "In Jesus' day the 'zealot' hope was expressed in the slogan 'No master except God'". Dr Barnett calls one zealot, Judas the Galilean, the Osama bin Laden of his day. He led a revolt in AD 6, when Jesus the Galilean was about ten years old.[12]

'No master except God' is a declaration in favour of

God's kingdom. Dangerous words; you could acquire a crown of thorns for announcing its imminence. Depending, of course, what you meant. Jesus, understandably, spent a lot of time explaining what *he* meant.

He certainly talked about the coming of the reign of God upon the earth. The coming of God's reign (as opposed to the kingdoms of men) is going to be cataclysmic. Furthermore, he called it by the dangerously ambiguous word 'gospel', or 'good news'.

On the one hand the word went back 700 years to the prophet Isaiah and his prediction that the Lord would come as King to his people. This he called 'gospel'. On the other hand, in the first-century world of the Roman Empire, it referred to the birth of a new heir to the throne or to the coming of the Emperor, both 'good news' events.

To call Jesus' announcement 'good news', therefore, was to suggest at least that there was going to be a competition for the throne, that here was a message political. When Jesus preached, conflict was in the air from the very beginning. No wonder he was crucified: that was a decisive answer to his pretensions.

There has been considerable scholarly discussion as to whether Jesus himself was a zealot, an insurrectionist. Sober historical research cannot sustain that. "My kingdom", he said to Pontius Pilate, "is not of this world" (John 18:36)—and it was this idea that he spent a lot of time explaining. The 'kingdom' language was not a call for political or military action as such. "Turn the other cheek" had a very contemporary application in those days. He clearly taught that the kingdom was a gift of God to be expected, but not as a product of human effort to be worked towards or brought in by violence. Not that these crucial distinctions seem to have done him much good; it was crucifixion for him.

Have you noticed that the closer we get to the Jesus of history, the more interesting but less relevant he seems? No wonder men such as Carlyle and his French contemporary Ernest Renan laid great stress on his ethics and his model life. What else were they to do with him? How else could you explain his influence?

When we approach the real Jesus, when we put him back into his times, we can understand him better. But he seems so particular that it becomes impossible to give him any universal significance. That is why his future has become problematic; because he spoke so much about what was to come.

What sense can we make of this?

He was a prophet of a kingdom, which he said was very near in time. Why on earth, then, are we still talking about him? Is it not time to shake off the cultural burden of a failed prophet, this pale Galilean as he has been called, and to seek fresh heroes, fresh gurus? Or, perhaps, to shake ourselves free from all who call on us to repent and believe? Surely Jesus has no future precisely because he thought so much about the future. His future did not come, it is past, he no longer matters. The wonder is that he has had any influence at all. Perhaps there is no contest between Jesus and rock 'n' roll.

To investigate these themes two ways open before us. The next chapter explores the 19th-century answer. Perhaps we can salvage something out of the teaching of Jesus, without having to accept his apocalyptic announcements? Or, perhaps, if we really understood him, we can finally rid ourselves of his kingdom, and reduce him to an ancient moral sage?

Or, then again, perhaps not.

2 | Jesus—religious genius or failed prophet?

Do you want this world to end and a new one to begin?

Rather surprisingly, the British and Australian Parliaments commence proceedings with such a prayer. It goes something like this:

> "Father, hallowed be your name. Your kingdom come. Give us each day our daily bread, and forgive us our sins, for we ourselves forgive everyone who is indebted to us. And lead us not into temptation." (Luke 11:2-4; cf. Matthew 6:9-13)

Here are some of the most famous words in history, known and prayed daily by millions of people. And yet do Jesus' followers realize that they are praying—among other things—for the end of the world?

Even though there is the intimate opening ("Father"), typical of Jesus but untypical of the religion of his day, the brevity (just five requests) and the absence of religious palaver (no monumental or mystical flattery of God, just the five short 'asks'), what are we really asking for? Only for an apocalyptic cataclysm.

Jesus assumed that we are very dissatisfied with the present state of affairs; that we can see the immense harm that human evil is doing to the world and in the world; that we want justice to be done at last; that we long for the present world order to cease and a new age to be ushered in; that we want to be there when it happens, even though we contribute to the evil; that we want the present world political system to give way to the kingdom of God; that we want the meek to inherit the earth.

We are saying, "Bring it on!"

Even praying for mundane things like daily bread is not as straightforward as it seems. An odd Greek word is used here that possibly means not our 'daily bread' but something more like 'tomorrow's bread'—in other words, let us eat today the bread which we will consume in the coming kingdom.

But if the Lord's Prayer has an ominous, apocalyptic edge to it, why do we continue to use it? More to the point, has all this fervent praying for the end of the world amounted to anything? Here is a demonstrable and monumental failure. How can we in all seriousness continue to pray for the end of the world—which hasn't happened?

So why bother with Jesus? Will he have any part to play in our future? Why should we take any notice of him? To answer this, it is necessary to give a picture of him as he was, and especially to explain what he was on about.

Earlier, I made the point that Jesus is often thought of today as though he was a sort of moral teacher, a source of values, perhaps even a religious genius. But in fact he was one who announced the immediate coming of God's kingdom. He was a prophet of the End, like a man with a sandwich board that says, "Repent, for the kingdom of God is at hand!" But if that is so, how did we come to think of him mainly as a moral teacher?

What happened was an enormous transformation of the view of Jesus, a legacy of the 18th and 19th centuries. When modern critical history was born, one of its first projects was to look at the Bible from the viewpoint of human reason. The Bible was no longer regarded as infallible; the miracles of Jesus were treated with scepticism; and his life was studied without the aura of divinity.

For example, in one highly influential 19th-century book, Ernest Renan's *The Life of Jesus,* Jesus became the man—but still only a man—who introduced true religion to the world, just as Socrates introduced philosophy, and Aristotle, science.[1]

Renan was a brilliant romantic stylist (if you like that sort of thing): "His [Jesus'] preaching", writes Renan, "was gentle and pleasing, breathing nature and the perfume of the fields. He loved the flowers, and took from them his most charming lessons. The birds of the heaven, the sea, the mountains, and the games of children furnished in turn the subject of his instructions."[2]

But there were no miracles. For Renan, it was the power of Jesus' personality that may have cured some from certain illnesses. Of his death, Renan gushes: "Rest now in thy glory, noble pioneer. Thy work is completed, thy divinity is established ... For thousands of years the world will extol thee."[3] As to the cause of his alleged resurrection, Renan attributes it to the impression he had made on his disciples, and especially Mary Magdalen: "Divine power of love! Sacred moments in which the passion of one possessed gave to the world a resuscitated God!"[4]

Of course Renan knew that Jesus' expectation of an apocalyptic kingdom of God was a problem. His approach was to see it merely as the outward form, the husk of Jesus' teaching. He concluded that, as far as the apocalyptic was concerned, Jesus was simply wrong, and shown to be wrong within a generation: "The world has not ended, as Jesus announced and as his disciples believed."[5]

Why then still bother with Jesus? A good question.

Renan made two key moves. He transferred the kingdom to the heart, and he made it the work of men: "... each one silently creates this kingdom by the true conversion of the heart", he says; it is "only the highest form of the good" ... "the reign of justice, which the faithful, according to their ability, ought to help in establishing ..."[6]

But not all were convinced.

I will never forget first reading the opening words of one of the most important books ever written about Jesus. The author lays it down that in the future:

… German theology will stand as a great, unique phenomenon in the mental and spiritual life of our time … And the greatest achievement of German theology is the critical investigation of the life of Jesus.[7]

The publication date was 1906, and the author was the famous and multi-talented Albert Schweitzer: philosopher, historian, theologian, musician, medical missionary, Nobel Peace Prize winner—and German. The book, in its English title, was *The Quest of the Historical Jesus.*

Schweitzer was highly critical of Renan. And he was right. What Schweitzer saw with great clarity was that the 19th-century re-translation of Jesus into a model moralist or even a religious genius was impossible. The futurist elements of Jesus' thought were not incidental; it was not a husk to be discarded in favour of the spiritual essence. Jesus was not enunciating a perennial philosophy; he was announcing a coming event. If the event did not occur, his authority as a teacher—and hence his morality and religion—must be destroyed.

Schweitzer's treatment of Renan was devastating: "There is scarcely any other work on the subject", he writes, "which so abounds in lapses of taste—and those of the most distressing kind … It is Christian art in the worst sense of the term—the art of the wax image. The gentle Jesus, the beautiful Mary, the fair Galileans who form the retinue of the 'amiable carpenter', might have been taken over in a body from the shop-window of an ecclesiastical art emporium …"[8]

But that leaves us with the original difficulty. I will put it as baldly as I can. If you approach Jesus as a mere figure of history—no miracles, no resurrection, no death for all mankind—and if you want to explain why he is so important, you have two options. With Renan you can leave history behind and simply re-package Jesus as a religious and moral teacher. Or, with Schweitzer, you can save history by seeing Jesus as a (failed) apocalyptic prophet. In other words, with Renan you can save Jesus, but lose your integrity; with Schweitzer you keep your integrity, but lose your Jesus.

If this is the choice, the honours go to Schweitzer. That was the verdict of the 20th century. Schweitzer, of course, did attempt to 'save' Jesus, but how to resurrect him remained the task of the 20th century. A rather galling fate for Jesus—to be saved and resurrected by academics, of all people.

After all the arguing what are we left with? Why should Jesus, a first-century failed prophet, be of any interest to us at all? It is hard enough now to understand why he had such a great past, let alone a future. And yet that is not fair. Jesus is better than that. After all, even an unbelieving HG Wells clearly regarded Jesus as the most dominant figure in all history in his history of the world. For this there must be a reason.

Recently I sat down and read the Gospels again. I invite you to try the same experiment, with, say, Luke, the third Gospel. What is very clear is that, at the very least, in Jesus we are dealing with a powerful mind and a strikingly original, prophetic voice.

Over and again, Jesus said things that are arresting, utterly memorable, challenging, penetrating, provocative and—I can think of no other description—simply true. He utters words full of consolation, words full of hope, words full of razor wire, words full of health, words full of wisdom. This immediately raises the problem again: if he was merely a failed prophet, why are his words so potent even today? I guess one reason is that he lived what he said.

We have no portrait of Jesus; we do not know what he looked like. We have no sound recording of the Sermon on the Mount; we do not know what his accent was like. We have no idea of his voice or gestures.

Presumably as a baby he had nappy rash and sore gums, and we know that he ate and drank and talked and slept and had a family and close friends and emotions, and that he touched people and took children on his knee, and that once his eyes looked at Peter after he denied him (a look that has been remembered ever since), and we know that he was crucified.

Without even a word-portrait, we have to look at him 'indirectly', so to speak. We look at his actions, his words. We observe how people reacted to him. We can say that he provoked very strong emotions. We see people responding to him with fear, anger, enmity; we see others crowding him, often amazed at something he has said or done; we see love for him, faith in him, passionate gratitude to him. He strikes me as having been an awkward, uncomfortable, demanding, liberating, inspiring, extraordinary leader. Indeed, he established, by word and deed, a fresh model of leadership—the strong but humble servant-leader—a model that has forever endowed service of others with honour, self-sacrifice with praise and undeserved love with glory.

"Greater love has no-one than this", said Jesus, "that someone lays down his life for his friends" (John 15:13). His insight at the same moment affronts our instinctive selfishness and compels our moral agreement. We know that he is right.

You catch a glimpse of something else in the responses of people. They were aware of a sort of moral otherness about him; don't get me wrong—love for others was so much part of his person that he was not a gloomy killjoy. But he set a standard for what humans could be like and somehow what God is like at the same time.

Not surprisingly, he crossed some of the toughest human boundaries to touch people and change their lives. He touched those with leprosy, he spoke with the despised, and entertained the outcast. An encounter with Jesus often led to transformation of life, a new liberty and joy, a sense of acceptance, of forgiveness. Often, but not always. Not everyone could pay the price, and one of his closest friends betrayed him to death.

Jesus often spoke in parables and it is these little masterpieces that help explain the riddle: if he was not a religious genius but a failed prophet, why has he been such a great success?

Parables are little choice-makers. They may or may not be stories, allegories or proverbs. But they reach out and pull us into the picture, show us for what we are, force on us a choice. A parable is a moral and spiritual device for sorting us out.

Take the most famous of all, in Luke 10:25-37. A lawyer asked Jesus how to inherit eternal life. Jesus forced the man to answer his own question: he must utterly love God and utterly love his neighbour. He riposted, "And who is my neighbour?" Jesus saw an evasion: did he really care who his neighbour was, or was he trying to avoid utter love?

Jesus' answer is a miniature masterpiece, a compressed, choice-making story, a similitude in which the lawyer is exposed, and then, to our dismay, so are we.

First, he sets it up:

> "A man was going down from Jerusalem to Jericho, and he fell among robbers, who stripped him and beat him and departed, leaving him half dead."

Then it becomes like a classic three-men-went-into-a-bar story:

> "Now by chance a priest was going down that road, and when he saw him he passed by on the other side. So likewise a Levite, when he came to the place and saw him, passed by on the other side. But a Samaritan, as he journeyed, came to where he was, and when he saw him, he had compassion. He went to him and bound up his wounds, pouring on oil and wine. Then he set him on his own animal and brought him to an inn and took care of him. And the next day he took out two denarii and

gave them to the innkeeper, saying, 'Take care of him, and whatever more you spend, I will repay you when I come back'."

The Samaritan had gone into compassion overdrive.

In those days, Samaritans and Jews were like the Protestants and Catholics of recent Belfast. They hated each other. So here's a nasty moment for the lawyer: "Which of these three, do you think, proved to be a neighbour to the man who fell among the robbers?" And note, the neighbour is not who we might expect; the helper is the neighbour.

In this amazing finale, Jesus does two things at once. He creates both verb and noun. He both shows what it is to be neighbour, and forces his questioner to admit that the Samaritans are neighbours. You can almost hear the clench in the voice of the lawyer as he avoids the word 'Samaritan' in his reply: "The one who showed him mercy". And then the stiletto-like words of Jesus—"You go, and do likewise". Be like a Samaritan, of all people.

This is a self-involving moral masterpiece. On its own it confirms the view of Jesus as the great teacher. The story has done immense good in human history; if this was the totality of the legacy of Jesus, it would be enough to establish his greatness.

This story in its context, however, also reminds us that Jesus is not a mere moralist. The original question of the lawyer was not "who is my neighbour?", but "what shall I do to inherit eternal life?"; that is, "what must I do to enter the kingdom of God, and so have life in the age to come?" It was a 'kingdom' question, a question of the end of all things, that created this story.

At one level, it shows us why Jesus was no failure. His powerful moral insights were powerful precisely because they put the present moment in touch with the future.

We tend to think that moral insights are mere values plucked from the air, perhaps inspired by an edifying tale such as the one about Simpson and his donkey saving the wounded at Gallipoli. Jesus, however, comes from the past with his words projecting into the future. They force us to examine the present in the light of what has been and what is yet to be. What Jesus shows us is that morality depends on a particular view of human nature and human destiny. If he is a master moralist it is because he understood both of these things. He understood who we are and where we are.

What did he say about that destiny, that coming kingdom?

The picture that Jesus painted of the end involved the great things we would all probably long for: the defeat of evil and the triumph of good; the death of death; a future of justice and yet forgiveness; intense, overflowing human happiness and joy. He called the coming kingdom a banquet, a wedding, a feast, a resurrection, a robust and loving community, in which every tear would be wiped away and we would live joyously as we were meant to, under the rule of the Father-God.

Mind you, entry into the kingdom would not be automatic. If there is to be a future without evil, something would have to be done with us. Jesus was completely clear-eyed about human nature; he did not regard it as inherently good and worthy of praise. He announced the kingdom in advance in order that we may repent. Integral to the healing power of forgiveness is the repentance that is necessary for it.

Even the coming judgement contains a sort of good news. It warns us that every word, thought and deed will be scrutinized on that day. Everything about you matters to God. In his words Jesus established our unique, individual significance.

And yet what of the crucial difficulty, that the kingdom he announced never arrived? That is the crux of the problem for Renan, for Schweitzer, and for us. To this Jesus would reply, "But that is not true. The kingdom has arrived."

> "With what can we compare the kingdom of God, or what parable shall we use for it? It is like a grain of mustard seed, which, when sown on the ground, is the smallest of all the seeds on earth, yet when it is sown it grows up and becomes larger than all the garden plants and puts out large branches, so that the birds of the air can make nests in its shade." (Mark 4:30-32)

The kingdom of heaven is not going to be a final big bang; instead, like a seed in the earth, it has now been inserted into history. For now it is a growth, not an earthquake. In other words, the kingdom has already come in essence, but it is still to come in completeness.

Once, having been asked when the kingdom of God would come, Jesus replied:

"The kingdom of God is not coming with signs to be observed, nor will they say, 'Look, here it is!' or 'There!' for behold, the kingdom of God is in the midst of you." (Luke 17:20-21)

The kingdom is both present and future.

It would be right to expect that Jesus would have to say and do a great deal more to convince us that the kingdom of God has already arrived, even in mustard seed proportions. And he did. He explained what he meant by God's kingdom and then he did something that, he believed, set it going. What he did I will discuss in the next chapter, but first we should consider what else Jesus said about the nature of the kingdom.

A number of Jesus' parables show what sort of kingdom the kingdom of God is—what its ethos is, what its king is like, what it is like to belong to this realm. If Jesus is right, I do not have to prove God's existence because he has already arrived in our midst. We are not dealing with our search for God, but with God's revelation of himself to us, through Jesus. The parables force us to ask: what are we going to do about this new historical reality?

Two particular parables out of any number address these issues. The first concerns the cost of the kingdom, the second concerns the membership of the kingdom.

"The kingdom of heaven is like a merchant in search of fine pearls, who, on finding one pearl of great value, went and sold all that he had and bought it." End of story (Matthew 13:45-46).

It doesn't have much of a plot really; it's not a story, it's an action. Furthermore, it seems like a foolish action; what is he now going to do with the pearl of such great price? Has he reduced himself to penury so that he may gaze on it? The parable has always irritated me with its extravagant, foolish behaviour.

But then as a 'choice-maker' it was intended to irritate. Jesus is provoking us: the kingdom of God is of such value that we should sell all we have to possess it; cross every boundary, pay any price, make any sacrifice; become fixated, focused, fanatical, obsessive, passionate. To an age which values cool, Jesus says value hot, make the kingdom everything or don't touch it at all. This is what Jesus means by "Repent!" To enter the kingdom demands a complete reorientation of life, from self to God and then to others. He makes it sound so hard; indeed it all sounds impossible. The cost is too high. Furthermore, the kingdom of God is going to be a highly moral place. We ask ourselves: how am I going to be included? Fortunately for you and me the way God runs his kingdom breaks all our preconceptions.

Here is a second 'choice-maker', with a word on that subject:

> He [Jesus] also told this parable to some who trusted in themselves that they were righteous, and treated others with contempt: "Two men went up into the temple to pray, one a Pharisee and the other a tax collector. The Pharisee, standing by himself, prayed thus: 'God, I thank you that I am not like other men, extortioners, unjust,

adulterers, or even like this tax collector. I fast twice a week; I give tithes of all that I get.' But the tax collector, standing far off, would not even lift up his eyes to heaven, but beat his breast, saying, 'God, be merciful to me, a sinner!' I tell you, this man went down to his house justified, rather than the other. For everyone who exalts himself will be humbled, but the one who humbles himself will be exalted." (Luke 18:9-14)

The Pharisee and the tax collector: a sharp, unforgettable message about who gets a place in the kingdom of God. It's important to realize that Pharisees were rightly admired for religious zeal and moral integrity. In fact, therefore, the parable illustrates one of the most disturbing elements of both the preaching and the activities of Jesus. He deliberately ate with those who stood no chance: the spiritually unclean, the morally unpleasant, the socially outcast. He offered them forgiveness and a welcome in his kingdom. He 'justified' the unjust ones, and forces us to identify either with the Pharisees or the tax collector.

To put it another way: although we are morally flawed and lost, God has mercy for us. God is Father to us; he is our Neighbour; he is the Good Samaritan to me and to you. We have no claim on him; we are like a wastrel son who ran away and became a prodigal; we are like a sheep that strayed and became utterly lost until the shepherd found it again; we are like a sick person who has found a great physician, a doctor for the sick soul; together, we are like a fractured family that at last has found its way home for Christmas.

So, to return to how I began this chapter: keep praying, Federal Parliament—you have got it right. You are praying both for the kingdom of God to be manifest at the end of history and inside history: "Your will be done on earth as it is in heaven", asks the Speaker. You are praying for God's justice, both now and then. Your prayer assumes that good things from the future kingdom have begun to grow in this world.

The kingdom has been introduced into the historical process, as Jesus claimed. In fact, many have been inspired to political and social transformation by the ideals of the kingdom which Jesus said was both present and future.

Remember my question: "Why was the apparent failure of Jesus such a success?" The answer is that he *did* introduce God's kingdom. So then, who was Jesus? Did he do miracles? How did he introduce the kingdom, if he did?

3 | Jesus—was he miraculous?

What do you think of Jesus?

Or try another question: what do you think of miracles? Possible? Impossible? Unlikely?

With the question of miracles we come to a highly significant fork in the road which will determine many of our personal attitudes to Jesus and to the Bible.

From the late 17th century onwards, historians and philosophers began to assume that Jesus should be assessed independently of the miraculous. Rigorous history had no more place for miracles than rigorous science. My guess is that, paradoxically, this attitude was in part the product of Protestant theology. In the 16th century, the Protestants made two moves that unintentionally fed into the scepticism of a later age.

The first Protestant move was to emphasize God's power. Protestants felt that much of established religion was an attempt to manipulate God. They regarded the teaching of the Catholic church as encouraging people to try and save themselves by their own good works.

For Protestants, God ruled the world all-powerfully, and ruled the world consistently and intimately. The one world moves under the control of the one sovereign will. Therefore saints and sacraments had no importance as intermediaries. The mercy of God encouraged humans to approach him directly through Jesus.

The thing that preserved the Protestant view was a powerful sense that God is our Father, that Jesus is our Saviour, and that the Holy Spirit lives in the heart of the believer. In short, it was a spiritual, relational religion. But if you take the religious heart out of Protestantism, you are left with a cool metaphysic.

Over time, the stress on the consistency of God came to be described by some in terms of immutable laws set up by God to run the world. This kept him at a welcome distance from the world. He was not an interventionist. And in this system you never asked God for anything in prayer; you acknowledged him by saying 'thank you'. The problem with miracles was that they allegedly broke God's unbreakable laws of nature. And as this is logically incoherent, there can be no miracles.

The second Protestant move was as a response to the frequently claimed miracles associated with Catholic shrines and saints. Such miracles seemed to validate the claims of the Catholic Church to authority. Protestants could have met these claims with stories of their own miracles, but on the whole they did not. Instead they denied virtually all miracles, except the ones in the Bible. As far as they were concerned, this made the miracles of Jesus all the more dramatic and wonderful. It helped keep the focus on Jesus.

As far as sceptical historians were concerned, however, it encouraged them to doubt all claims to miracles whatsoever. After all, if the laws of nature are virtually unbreakable, which is more likely—that a miracle has occurred or that the observer is wrong or lying? In these terms, there is never a report of a miracle sufficiently persuasive for you to believe. It is not that miracles are impossible; they are just implausible. How could there ever be enough evidence to believe in one? Such an argument is associated, of course, with the name of the great Scottish philosopher and historian David Hume.

This conclusion created a major cultural problem. Apart from the fact that, throughout history and in the contemporary world as well, many people have claimed experience of the supernatural in the form of a miracle, what do historians do with Jesus if miracles cannot appear on the agenda?

Broadly speaking, apart from complete loss of faith in Christianity, three responses developed. *First*, the stories about Jesus and his miracles were regarded as pious frauds. The disciples had invented them to boost the product, so to speak.

The *second* response was to regard the miracle-tales as a combination of misunderstanding and the seductive effects of a powerful personality. Did Jesus walk on water? No, he was walking on a sandbank just under the water. Did he feed a great crowd with meagre provisions? No, but he so shamed those who had brought their lunch with them, that they shared what they had with those who had nothing. Did he rise from the dead? No, but it seemed as though he had because he was in a deep coma when he was buried, and awoke as if from death itself. Did he heal the sick? No, but such was the power of his personality that he brought help to those with psychosomatic illnesses.

The *third* response invoked the category of 'myth'. 'Myth' is a complex word, but some myths at least function to tell the truth through stories: the stories may or may not have much connection with historical truth, but that is not what marks them out as mythical. What does this is their explanatory power. For example, the military campaign at Gallipoli was a real event, but it is sometimes referred to as 'the Gallipoli myth' because of the way the story is used to define or explain the Australian character.

Thus, in the terms of the 'myth response', to ask whether Jesus walked on water is to miss the point. You may say that it is utterly impossible, but the author probably never intended us to believe this literally. It was his or her way of showing the divinity of Jesus. Likewise the resurrection stories are merely the outward mythic garb, intended to tell us that Jesus is still alive.

Some modern authors write as though they have invented one or another of these approaches to the miracles themselves. In fact, all three responses had developed by the 1830s. They continue to have their scholarly advocates, although in recent times the last is the most popular.

It is at this point that we arrive at the fork in the road I mentioned at the beginning of this chapter.

It is obvious that much historical writing about Jesus is clearly shaped by whether or not the author believes in the possibility of the miraculous. Your attitude to Jesus depends on whether you think that the Gospel miracles— or some of them—are likely to have occurred.

But are people today committed to be sceptical about miracles? Must we accept the view that they are either impossible or implausible? I believe that the answer is 'no' for three main reasons.

First, the philosophical mood has shifted somewhat. Talk of 'unbreakable laws of nature' depends on a certain view of God. But it is not the only possible view of God. The old definition of miracles did not make miracles impossible except by definition.

We are not bound to define miracles in the old way or to think that the remote non-interventionist God is the true God. The God of Jesus is certainly not remote. His God rules all things in a constant, consistent and direct manner, and reveals himself to us in his Word. (Today we call this 'theism'.) We may, if we wish, call this consistency a 'law of nature'. But God is able to vary his habitual actions on occasion for his own good and wise reasons. Thus, normally, God does not resurrect dead persons. He directs the world in a way in which this does not happen. But there is nothing to stop him bringing about a resurrection if he so chooses. He certainly has the power to do it. We live in a personal, not an impersonal universe.

Thus philosopher Dr Bruce Langtry of Melbourne University uses the following definition of a miracle:

> An event is a miracle brought about by God, wholly or partially without the mediation of causal powers given by God to created persons and objects.[1]

In these terms, we could develop a coherent philosophy not only quite consistent with the Bible, but with modern science and with historical research. It would not validate all claims, but it would not rule them out either. In short, whether you are open to the idea of miracles depends on what sort of God you start with.

Furthermore, the idea that critical science and history only developed in opposition to Christianity is a philosophical and historical mistake. I would argue the contrary case: that Christian theism was at least congenial—indeed perhaps it was necessary—to the development of modern science and history.

I agree, of course, that both science and history in their normal operational mode make no provision for miracles.

This is a working assumption, indispensable to these specific fields of knowledge. But great as these disciplines are, they are limited by their working assumptions. In particular they find unique or rare events difficult to assimilate, but miracles *are* rare events. Their rarity doesn't automatically discount their existence. As with other rare or unique events we are still committed to examining the evidence. For example, a person who claims to be an eyewitness to a miracle can rightly be interrogated without any necessary presumption that they are lying or have been deceived. We should be able to trust in good evidence. It's just that for miracles the bar has been, rightly or wrongly, set higher.

Science tells us what can and cannot occur, provided that we assume that the system under study is a causally closed one. But no branch of science has discovered by empirical investigation that the physical universe *is* a causally closed system; that is, that nothing affects it that is not a part of it.

If we accept theism as plausible, much of the case against miracles takes up its tent and steals quietly away. Even an atheist can logically admit the possibility of miracles, if he or she is prepared to concede even one chance in twenty that theism is true. Of course this does not demonstrate that any particular miracle has taken place. But we may be rationally far more open to the possibility than has been the case in previous generations because it no longer seems intellectually indefensible.

I can chart the process in my own experience. When I began my serious study of theology almost 40 years ago, the philosophical ethos was overwhelmingly hostile to theism. The only ally that Protestants like me seemed to have was existentialism—a dangerous friend at best. One of the formidable foes of theism at the time was philosophy Professor Antony Flew of Reading University in the United Kingdom.

I don't suggest that the mainstream has shifted to theism. But there are now significant philosophers who have created space at the table for belief in such a God. Interestingly, the fearsome Professor Flew now appears to be flirting with theism—certainly not Christianity, but no longer atheism.

Second, there is the nature of the New Testament itself. I don't think it is possible to give an historically plausible account of how the early Christian movement developed, and how the New Testament was written, on the assumption that we are dealing with fraud or misunderstanding or myth. Reputable historians are divided on this matter, but that is my critical judgement in the light of the evidence as I have assessed it.

And I am not alone. I recall Professor CFD Moule of Cambridge University drawing attention to the indisputable fact of the existence and nature of the Christian church from the period immediately after Jesus. He then pertinently asked that if this fact "rips a great hole in history, a hole the size and shape of Resurrection, what does the secular historian propose to stop it up with?"[2]

(More recently, Bishop Tom Wright of Durham has written massively, persuasively and positively about the bodily resurrection of Jesus.[3] Once you can see that there is no *a priori* argument that renders miracles impossible or even implausible, his is a case to answer.)

The 'myth' classification simply doesn't fit in with the way we see the New Testament authors actually handling their own historical sources and their emphasis on eyewitnesses—and the explanations about handy sandbanks and generous crowds are somehow harder to believe than the miracle tales themselves.

I know that my conclusions about Jesus would be utterly different if I did not believe in a God fully capable of miraculously healing the sick and raising the dead. But I do. I think miracles *are* possible and that changes everything.

Third, there is the significance of Jesus in our estimate of the miracles. His words were remarkable, and his words and his miracles actually hang together. In line with Old Testament expectations, he spoke of a coming kingdom in which the world would be renewed, evil put to flight, the sick healed, the prisoners released, the poor cared for and the hungry fed. The point is that if anyone could do miracles, Jesus would be that person.

His miracles embodied the kingdom of God. To assess them fairly you must ask why they occurred. They were not mere wonder-works, magicians' tomfoolery, charismatic ego-trips or demonstrations intended to silence sceptics about the supernatural; they were experiences of the world to come, reflecting the very abundance and grace of the Father-God about whom he preached. To that extent they are mythological but they are found at the point at which myth and truth kiss. The truth embodies and transcends the myth.

It is here, then, that we may part company, intellectually at least. You may decide that miracles as such are impossible and so, without further ado, you may say that while the teaching of Jesus is remarkable, he is indeed a failed prophet, and of marginal interest in the years ahead.

For me, however, accepting that miracles are at least possible, I must continue to explore whether Jesus is a success or a failure. But even I have to admit that crucifixion would normally be regarded as a particularly dismal failure. It was the rejection of him as a king.

John the Baptist was not crucified, but he certainly had a famous way of dying. His severed head was presented to Queen Herodias after her daughter had danced for the king. Some dance; some gift!

John was the cousin and forerunner of Jesus. He too preached the coming of the kingdom of God. He was also murdered in a political assassination. But no-one suggested that he was any more than a prophet of the kingdom; he did not have a personal role in it.

Jesus, on the other hand, said that *he* did.

Jesus had a linguistic trick of using the phrase 'Son of Man', usually to refer to himself. Interestingly it hardly survived in his lifetime. When the first generation of Christians spoke about him, they reported him using the term, but they did not much employ it themselves, another indication of their care as witnesses.

'Son of Man'? It can mean 'man', but that does not cover all the uses. It has the ring of an office, an official position, about it. It does not mean 'Messiah' or 'King'. And yet its use seems almost certain to be part of Jesus' beliefs about the coming kingdom of God and the end of all things.

Most scholars rightly see the term 'Son of Man' originating in the book of the prophet Daniel in the Old Testament. In chapter seven of that book, there is the prediction of four fierce earthly kingdoms. But the fifth kingdom, the kingdom of God, is given to "one like a son of man". Daniel seems to think of this Son of Man as the whole people of God, who are given an eternal dominion. By using it of himself, Jesus puts himself personally at the centre of God's future plans for his kingdom, as if he has become the representative of all people.

It's an obscure reference, but Jesus fostered a degree of mystery, of reticence, about himself. A bold public claim to be the Messiah (or 'Christ') would have led to his early demise, and in any case would have created false expectations about what he was trying to achieve. 'Son of Man' language still makes a surprising but very impressive claim for authority.

It also sharply raises the question: what connection did Jesus see between himself and the kingdom that he was announcing?

We can discern something of the nature of this connection from the following. Not only did he call himself the 'Son of Man', but when he was asked about the timing of the coming of the kingdom, he replied, "… the kingdom of God is in the midst of you" (Luke 17:21). According to the Gospel writers, he once privately asked his disciples, "Who do you say that I am?" and accepted the reply that he was the Christ, the Son of the living God, a royal title (Matthew 16:15-16).

But what are we to make of his claim that "there are some standing here who will not taste death until they see the kingdom of God after it has come with power" (Mark 9:1)? Surely that was not proved true; surely it is here we see his failure as a prophet. After all, he was crucified; then, as now, that spells failure.

Crucifixion. Of its grotesque and fearful nature I need say little. The Romans were masters of the art of punishment as public propaganda. The shameful agonies of the victims—though suffered in public view—were so obscene that mention of them was forbidden in polite society. We think of crucifixion as a static death, but perhaps it was more like a slowly moving death, as the victim struggled for air, pulling himself up and then collapsing, until he could move no more.

Why would anyone invent a religion centred on a

crucified man? It posed immense difficulties for the first Christian missionaries, since their Scriptures explicitly cursed anyone who hangs on "a tree". So we can imagine what the masses made of the story or any claim that this was somehow the kingdom of God come in power. There is, in fact, some striking evidence of popular derision about worshipping a crucified man. One is a famously spiteful graffito from the second century, which depicts a crucified man with an ass's head, another man with his hand upraised, and beneath it the scrawl, "Alexamenos worships god".

The Gospel records of the death of Jesus have been subjected to as much research as any event in history. There remain outstanding questions about the arrest and trial and the responsibility of the different actors in the scene. The blame attached to the Jewish people as a whole for such a tragedy is utterly reprehensible, tragic and unhistorical. Jesus was, after all, himself a Jew.

The death of Jesus was clearly connected with an alleged claim to be a king. Nailed to his cross was an inscription which read something like this: "This is the King of the Jews" (Luke 23:38). 'Son of Man' language, reports of miracles, kingdom-of-God talk, an attack on the temple—it all added up to a case against him.

But—to state the obvious—the death of other insurrectionists at the same time is a mere footnote in history. We are fortunate even to know their names. What makes the death of Jesus one of the best-known facts in history? It is still commemorated in unnumbered sacramental meals week in week out, day in day out; the cross is still a sign better known than the golden arches.

I think that we are dealing here with three things: the *meaning* of his death; the *manner* of his death; and the *sequel* to his death.

First the *meaning*: there is no evidence that Jesus was a political rebel, aiming to overthrow Roman rule and set himself up as a king in Jerusalem or anywhere else. The idea has, of course, been rightly suggested, rightly tested and rightly dismissed.

Jesus understood that judicial death was a likely outcome of his activities. But his teaching was pacific and his disciples were not a guerrilla group. In one of the most famous scenes in the Gospels, he was challenged about whether to pay taxes to Caesar or not. A highly loaded enquiry. He pointed to the head of Caesar on the currency and said, "Render to Caesar the things that are Caesar's, and to God the things that are God's" (Matthew 22:21). Given the vital role played by taxation in the empire, this was not the speech of a mutineer or political activist.

Yes, the kingdom of heaven would be a great transformation. But it had to come from the hand of God, not from the efforts of men. The kingdom he preached about was to be accepted, received, obeyed, prayed for—but not built, fought for or created. Except, in a sense, by him.

For others, crucifixion was the end to their career as a rebel. Yet Jesus saw his death as somehow the pivot of the kingdom; its fundamental precondition; the flashing forth of the divine judgement that was to precede its establishment. Thus in the Passover meal he shared with his disciples before his death, he makes this promise:

> "I have earnestly desired to eat this Passover with you before I suffer. For I tell you I will not eat it until it is fulfilled in the kingdom of God." (Luke 22:15-16)

The Passover, in which lambs were slaughtered to create safety for the people of Israel, is to be fulfilled in his sacrificial death.

Human beings have always gropingly sought to find peace and power in and with the universe through sacrifice. Sacrifice of animals, of food, of people, of children; the sacrifice of ourselves, our money, our time; even the gifts of our good works and our religion.

All this is shown up, and summed up and made obsolete, in Jesus' sacrifice. Wherever the sacrifice of Christ is truly trusted, animal and human sacrifice ceases.

Second, the *manner* of his death: in Luke's version of his death, there are two events that have always deeply moved me. They help explain why the crucifixion somehow expresses God's love.

At the time of his crucifixion Jesus prayed for God's forgiveness on those who crucified him: "Father, forgive them, for they know not what they do" (Luke 23:34). He lived and died enacting God's forgiveness on those who most needed a new heart and a new start in life. His death brought—and still brings—a sense of forgiveness.

There was another crucified at the same time who recognized his own faults, recognized the innocence of the man dying beside him, recognized that he was dying beside a dying king, and said to Jesus: "Remember me when you come into your kingdom". Jesus replied: "Today you will be with me in Paradise" (Luke 23:42-43). He was saying that this was not the end of his kingdom; it is the beginning of it, and it has room even for a man like you.

Little wonder Jean-Jacques Rosseau, no friend of Christianity, said:

> The life and death of Socrates are those of a philosopher;
> the life and death of Jesus are those of a God.

As an astonishing but incontestable fact, the kingdom of Jesus did come. His crucifixion was not a portal to oblivion, but to glory. That is, within a short time of his death and with ever-growing intensity, his followers began preaching that a crucified man was the Christ, and inviting men and women to attach themselves to him with a loyalty surpassing their loyalty to any person or state. And, in ever-increasing numbers, so they did. Since the death of Jesus there has always been a kingdom of Jesus in the world, if not a kingdom of God.

For a time it seemed that Christianity would confine itself within Judaism. In much of the New Testament, you can still see the signs of the original great debate in the new movement. Was it going to be for everyone, all on the same simple terms and conditions, or was it to be for the Jewish people only?

So the decision that Christianity was to be for everyone was momentous; it flowed from all that Jesus had said and, in particular, how he died. It turned Christianity into a world movement. It was not so much a new religion as a new and extraordinary empire, based on the possibility of peace with God through the death of Jesus. The Roman Empire did not become Christian because the Emperor did; it would be truer to say that the Emperor became Christian because his subjects did.

Now the *sequel*: the announcement of God's kingdom is really a declaration that the old age is passing and a new age has begun. The Jewish expectation of such an age included the hope that death would be defeated in a general resurrection of the dead. If the death of Jesus was not a mere failure but somehow the institution of the kingdom of God, you would look for resurrection. And indeed his disciples 'bore witness' that he had risen from the dead, as he said he would. Fundamentally, it is the evidence of these eyewitnesses that we rely on for our conviction that he rose from the dead. According to them, his tomb was unexpectedly empty. Neither they, nor their opponents, produced the body of Jesus to refute the claim of the empty tomb. Furthermore, according to them, he ate and drank with them in the kingdom of God. The sincerity of their witness was tested by martyrdom. They may have been wrong but they were themselves convinced of what they saw and heard. Something happened, and it was significant enough to change the world. Christians say it was the resurrection.

Of course, such a resurrection is a miracle, but if *a priori* you do not believe in miracles, then you will deny the resurrection in principle. For you, Jesus lies buried still; no new age has begun; the kingdom of Jesus and the kingdom of God are not the same thing at all. No kingdom of God has arrived. No amount of evidence—and it is interesting to investigate the matter from the point of view of evidence—would ever convince you. From this point of view, despite all the positive signs we have noted along the way, Jesus would appear to fall at the last hurdle. He is indeed a failed prophet, placed back in his tomb by modernity. The dust which he has become lies there still.

Of course, if the resurrection is credible, then the other miracles recorded in the Gospels are just as likely to be plausible. This would mean, too, that we do not live in a closed universe but an open one. For me—and I speak very personally—it is the difference between living in a black-and-white world and a world of colour.

In my judgement Jesus is not a failed prophet, but vindicated and successful. He predicted the coming of God's kingdom, and then he brought it in.

I agree the whole matter revolves inexorably around the question of what each of us makes of Jesus. But that is, after all, one of the key things about this discussion: I cannot make the judgement in your place. We must all read the Gospels and answer for ourselves the very question that he put to his disciples: "Who do you say that I am?"

4 | Jesus or Caesar— the choice of martyrs

Professor James Haire tells the following story from a time of community violence in East Indonesia:

> He [the pastor] knew that his case was hopeless. He asked to be allowed to pray. His wish was granted. He put on his preaching gown and knelt by the communion table. He prayed for his church, for his nation, for his congregation, and for those about to kill him. The Sunday School children, who observed the whole incident, told me what happened. Then he stretched his head forward and was beheaded. His head was carried on a pole around the village. His body was dragged by the feet for all to see.[1]

This story is both ancient and modern.

The pastor's blood is still fresh; some of the children are probably still in Sunday School.

"He prayed for those about to kill him ..." The pastor was deliberately following an ancient model. The first Christian martyr was Stephen. Here is how the Bible records his dying words:

> And as they were stoning Stephen, he called out, "Lord Jesus, receive my spirit". And falling to his knees he cried out with a loud voice, "Lord, do not hold this sin against them". And when he had said this, he fell asleep. (Acts 7:59-60)

Stephen prayed to Jesus and Stephen called him 'Lord'.

This was a revolution. Jesus preached the kingdom of God; then he claimed to have established it; then his followers claimed to belong to it. For Stephen at one end of history and for the pastor at the other, he was "Christ, the Lord". He inspired them to die; he inspired them *how* to die.

The word 'Lord' was not an empty title. Men and women were martyred, not for an idea but for a person. In an age where servants were commonplace, they called themselves his servants. They obeyed him, they entrusted themselves to him, even in death.

At irregular intervals over the next several hundred years, Christians were put to death for their faith. Indeed, one reason for the growing popular acceptance of Christianity in Roman times was that torture and death would not shake their allegiance to Jesus.

From that time, Christians have often been persecuted and murdered for their faith—and they still are. It's worth remembering that the greatest mass murderers of history were 20th-century atheists. Their blood-soaked century included Christians, as well as many others, as its victims. But Christians are not the only martyrs. Sometimes Christians have martyred others in a shocking travesty of the faith that they professed.

Martyrdom is sometimes questionable rather than admirable. It may, for example, be associated with terror and suicide-bombers. It makes us cling all the more to a liberal vision of society, in which we value tolerance, coolness, personal freedom, choice. We are rightly suspicious of any movement that demands this ultimate commitment. No-one can claim to be acting for Christ who martyrs someone else; no-one can claim to be acting for Christ who seeks to become a martyr; no-one can claim to be a martyr who harms others in becoming one. Sacrifice on behalf of others, where unavoidable, is one thing—fanatical suicide is another.

Three things led to the martyrdom of Christians in the ancient world. *First*, there was the extraordinary and exclusive claim by Jesus on the loyalty of his followers. Jesus had different images for this call he made; for example, when he said to one man, "Follow me", the man replied:

> "Lord, let me first go and bury my father." And Jesus said to him, "Leave the dead to bury their own dead. But as for you, go and proclaim the kingdom of God." (Luke 9:59-60)

Luke also records these uncompromising words:

> "If anyone would come after me, let him deny himself and take up his cross daily and follow me. For whoever

would save his life will lose it, but whoever loses his life for my sake will save it." (Luke 9:23-24)

"Take up his cross daily" is not then the crisis of final death, but the daily death of submission to the directions of another, to Jesus. There is no hint here, let me stress, of self-flagellation or other ascetic practices. Jesus is asking us to trust him, and follow his teaching, which is far harder and far better. We are, to use another image of his, 'yoked' to him. No wonder he said that before we enter his kingdom, we must count the cost.

Why did anyone accept discipleship under these terms? If we listen to the new disciples themselves, a fundamental reason was this: Jesus persuaded them that, through him, God was expressing his love and forgiveness, and that the death of Jesus proved and secured this. They were also convinced that he had risen from the dead. No resurrection, no kingdom.

They said that they loved him because he loved them. He demonstrated his love by dying for them. From the beginning, the death of Jesus has been the central inspiration of the citizens of his kingdom. It is a kingdom based on a love which transforms lives. Forgiveness has that power. Martyrdom, then, is only the ultimate form of obedience, of being a follower of Jesus. The cross is a daily pattern of life.

Second, martyrdom arose as the result of a serious dispute that engaged the early Christians. They had to decide this issue: was Jesus for the Jewish people only or was he for everyone? Now obviously, most Jewish people never accepted Jesus, but among those who did there was a crisis in their practise of Judaism. The problem was what to do about the non-Jewish believers. Like Judaism, the new gospel attracted a significant number of Gentiles who appreciated the high moral standards of the Jewish people and their beliefs about God. Were these converts to become Jews in order to be disciples or were they to be treated purely as believing Gentiles?

The final answer was momentous. It stopped the Christians from becoming a heretical sect within the broad scope of Judaism and put Christianity outside it, basically enabling it to become a world faith. The answer was that both Jews and Gentiles were accepted by God on identical terms—through faith in Jesus alone. The Jewish believers could keep some distinguishing features such as circumcision and their food laws, but they were not to impose these practices on the new Gentile believers, and the practices were not compulsory for Jewish believers either. This, Christians believed, was the true meaning of the Old Testament, the Hebrew Scriptures.

The Christian movement became not a nation, or a sprig of a nation, but an international movement among all the nations, with a profound sense of spiritual equality, between men and women, slaves and free, Jews and Gentiles. To this day, at the simplest of levels, if you wish to say what is the difference between Christianity and Judaism, it is this: Christianity affirms that Jesus is the

Christ, the fulfilment of the promises to Israel. Judaism denies it. Here indeed is a fork in the road, a choice with considerable ramifications.

Tragically, Christianity and Judaism are still divided by this question. But Christians true to their faith will honour the Jewish people, reject any persecution of them, mourn over their suffering, and seek good relations with the faith from which Christianity has emerged.

Third, martyrdom arose because the Christians' experience of the love of God through Jesus drove them to be missionaries. From its very inception, Christianity has been a missionary faith. It offers a message applicable to all: "For God so loved the world, that he gave his only Son ..." (John 3:16). Their basic message was that Jesus is Lord of all, to the exclusion of all rivals. We can understand what consternation this caused. Their mission drew them into protracted conflict with both pagan culture and the Roman Empire.

Take the pagans. Like our own, the ancient pagan world was pluralistic. The notable French historian Professor Veyne calls paganism 'free enterprise' religion:

> Each man was free to found his own temple and preach whatever god he liked, just as he might open an inn or peddle a new product. And each man made himself the client of whichever god he chose ...

Elsewhere he observes, "the gods of all people are true gods ... To take a special interest in one god was not to deny the others."[2] Christianity, however, did.

As far as the Roman Empire was concerned, religion was used to create loyalty. The step up from being an emperor to being a god was not a large one. Yet the Christians claimed that in Jesus they had a Lord who was higher than any other power in heaven or earth, and who demanded the prior loyalty of his followers in any contest with the state. They refused to allow that the state, or indeed any human authority, could be an absolute. Christianity taught that its followers had to obey the state, that state authority came from God. But it made the state relative, not absolute—and this was its offence against the Empire.

In short, their message affronted many Jewish people whose expectations of God's kingdom and understanding of God's king were rather different; it was laughable to the cultured and the uncultured in the pagan world; and it seemed to pose a political threat to Rome with its emphasis, so its critics said, on "another king, Jesus" (Acts 17:6-7).

Some hint of these difficulties comes from an early Christian missionary who wrote that his message about a crucified messiah was "a stumbling block to Jews and folly to Gentiles ..." (1 Corinthians 1:23). Frankly, it did not much look like what we mean by a religion. The choice it offered was so stark that its followers were often called atheists.

Here is the report of an encounter between an elderly bishop, Polycarp of Smyrna in Asia Minor, and the puzzled but inflexible Roman Proconsul. The date is somewhat after AD 150. The offence of Polycarp was to refuse to say "Caesar is Lord" and to sacrifice to the divinity of the Emperor:

> The Proconsul tried to persuade him to deny his faith, urging, "Have respect to your old age", and the rest of it according to the customary form, "Swear by the genius of Caesar; change your mind: say, 'Away with the Atheists'" … The Proconsul continued insisting and saying, "Swear, and I release you. Curse Christ." And Polycarp said, "Eighty-six years have I served Him, and He has done me no wrong: how can I blaspheme my King who saved me?"[3]

He belonged to two kingdoms, as do all Christians, and could not serve both equally. Polycarp was put to death.

The exact legal reason for the harassment of Christians by the Romans remains a matter of dispute. Nonetheless, there is no doubt that at the heart of it, as here, there was a fundamental clash of loyalties, a clash of lords.

Proper religious observance was thought to be essential to the wellbeing of the state. In a polytheistic—and hence pluralistic—world, an alternative kingdom had been born and was marketing itself vigorously. The problem was that it focused on Jesus as the exclusive—because inclusive—Lord of all.

Hence the Proconsul invites Polycarp to say, "Away with the Atheists". The 'atheists' were the Christians, since they were unbelievers in all but one God. Furthermore, the Christian movement did not respect political or social boundaries; it bound together in a committed way Jew, Greek, barbarian, slave, free, men and women. It was becoming something like a shadow of the Empire.

Despite the pluralism of paganism and the political power of Rome, Jesus persuaded an ever-increasing number of men and women that their best interests lay in deep commitment to him and to one another. In fact, the members of his kingdom were united in something called 'church'. And to that somewhat provocative word we now turn.

Cynics have observed that Jesus announced a kingdom, but all that emerged was a church.

Today, the word 'church' signifies a building, a profession, a worldwide institution, a liturgical activity, an ecclesiastical counterpart to the state. In common speech it generally refers to gorgeously arrayed pomposities engaged in arcane rituals and vaguely left-wing politics. Well may we say, God save the Church!

But the church of Jesus Christ did not enter history like that. The word 'church', in Greek *ekklesia*, seems to be largely derived from a political context. Every city had its 'church' or *ekklesia*, its municipal assembly or meeting. Christians took over this terminology for their own gatherings.

'Church' did not mean a huge international institution. The references were local. Its underlying sense was of a 'gathering', 'assembly', 'congregation', perhaps even a 'community'. The Jewish people in many of the ancient towns had the synagogue, a weekly local gathering for instruction and fellowship. The Christians called their synagogue 'church'. The choice of word created little comment. For a long time they had no specially dedicated buildings. Indeed the idea of sacred space, of statues and special objects of veneration, of ritual, of sacrifice, of sacrificing priests, of altars, was foreign to them.

The Christians seemed to their contemporaries more like a debating group strong on community than what we would call a religious cult. The new faith was a set of relationships rather than a religion.

What created a church? Missionaries would come and preach about Jesus and his kingdom. Some scoffed; some hesitated; others believed. The believers were formed into small regular meetings or *ekklesiai*. Each one was 'an *ekklesia* belonging to Jesus Christ'—presumably to distinguish it from the Jewish synagogue.

Unlike pagan religions, churches were strong on teaching. They were told that one God, the Father, was the creator of the world; that Jesus was the Son of God; that his death was redemptive and from it flowed forgiveness of sins; and that in trusting in Jesus as their Lord, they would receive forgiveness and the gift of the Holy Spirit. On the basis of that message, they were supposed to show three classic traits: first, faith, or trust in God and his Son Jesus the Christ; second, a righteous love—love for one another of course, but also love for all, including enemies; third, hope, directed towards the promises for the future made by Jesus.

The churches were products of the kingdom that Jesus had let loose on the world. To the ancients this did not look religious. There was a commitment of love towards other believers elsewhere. It was as if there was one overarching Church which found expression in many local churches, and yet each one was fully 'church' in its own right.

I believe that it is true to say that we see here the birth of something new, just as astronomers might observe the birth of a new star. Professor Veyne makes this key distinction:

> The pagans modelled relations with their gods on the political and social relations among themselves. It was the Christians who substituted the paternal model, basing relations with God on relations within the family, which is why Christianity, unlike Paganism, would be a religion of obedience and love.[4]

Professor Wayne Meeks of Yale says:

> Those odd little groups in a dozen or so cities of the Roman East were engaged, though they would not have put it quite this way, in constructing a new world. In time, more time than they thought was left, their ideas, their images of God, their ways of organizing life, their rituals, would become part of a massive transformation, in ways they could not have foreseen, of the culture of the Mediterranean basin and of Europe.[5]

Professor Judge of Macquarie University makes the same point. Christianity in the ancient world was "an intellectual movement of massive proportions and many ramifications". It was explicitly not like the ancient cults or, as we would call them, 'religions'. He observes:

By asserting the right to think and live differently within a common state, even to "form associations against the laws for the sake of the truth" ... the New Testament "assemblies" forged vital principles of our historical development. It is to them that we can trace the roots of the engaged, self-criticizing society that has generated the distinctive intellectual and political openness of the West.[6]

How did Christianity succeed in growing from a tiny and obscure group based on a crucified man to a movement capable of taming an empire?

A recent book by American sociologist Rodney Stark of Washington University points, for example, to the superior role of women in Christian communities; to the respect for life and the abhorrence of abortion and infanticide; to better fertility rates; to the way in which Christian teaching addressed the needs and fears of ordinary people; to the path of virtue that Christianity set people on; to the sense of hope that it gave them; to the way in which the practical love of the Christians, especially in times of emergency such as plagues, won the approval of their neighbours and actually improved their own life span.

Stark writes:

Christianity served as a revitalization movement that arose in response to the misery, chaos, fear and brutality of life in the Graeco-Roman world ...[7]

The Christians created little self-sustaining families out of strangers and enemies. He points out that mercy and pity were regarded as character defects in the ancient world, but that Judaism and Christianity taught otherwise. As

Jesus both modelled the love of God and taught the love of God, so men and women learned that love and pity were strengths, not weaknesses.

It was the Christians who stayed behind in the plagues to nurse the sick. It was the Christian sick who had a better chance of survival. So, too, did all, since the Christians nursed believers and unbelievers alike.

But why were they like this, when pity and mercy were not valued as character traits but regarded as weaknesses? It was the influence of Jesus. He ruled the hearts of his followers 'from the cross' so to speak, for it was by his death that he demonstrated that God is love. The very thing that made it impossible that he should be the earthly king was what made him Lord. It gave him followers who sacrificed for him, as he had for them.

This required, however, the completely counter-cultural assertion that he was the unique Lord of all. Pluralism in the ancient world was no more accepting of such a claim than it is today.

I have given a somewhat idealized picture of 'church' in its origins, but what of my present experience of church? I guess that I am as disappointed with church as anyone. It's hard to be reconciled to it sometimes. My fellow-believers often fail; they behave in ways that bring the name of Jesus into disrepute. They can be petty, quarrelsome and uncaring.

To tell the truth, I'm like that myself. Jesus has set up a model for life which is far beyond my capacity to keep.

It is just as well that Christianity is not a religion that requires me to create the kingdom of God through the goodness of my life. I am expected to orient my life to God in repentance, to make Jesus the Lord of my life, but I receive the kingdom of God as a gift. And its greatest gift is forgiveness, which is certainly my greatest need.

Despite my disappointment with the church, however, it's the sort of disappointment you may experience with any family. My church, and here I am not talking about the big institution but my *local* church, again and again fulfils my expectations. It is a place where I can find talk about Jesus that inspires genuine faith, hope and love. And I have received so much from others in the church that I could never repay.

Traditional Christendom may have collapsed and the denominations may be weak, but individual churches, congregations and communities are still there in their thousands in Australia, and they still intend to provide us with a family that transcends and enriches our personal families. As long as that experience continues to be available, the Christian faith retains a powerful presence.

More, I believe that such congregations continue to play a vital role in our community, as they have always done. At their best they give us little islands of faith, hope and love, turned out towards their community, and doing voluntarily a thousand things that our nation needs for its good health. And, even weakened as they might be, the denominations are similarly doing good work in the name of Jesus.

Compared to what such churches are actually doing, individualism is selfishness masquerading under the grand name of liberalism. Every Australian should be concerned about the loss of our faith communities.

Furthermore, if Meeks, Judge and Stark are right, Christianity brought something new and significant into the world through those little meetings called 'churches'. Like the kingdom of God that gave them birth, they existed within the political structures created by men to rule the world, supporting them, but with a loyalty beyond them.

They existed across nations and ethnic groups. They existed to educate their members on the upright life. They bound their members to one another by love, inspired not by airy talk about values, but by one of the greatest lives ever lived and by a unique death.

Over time, such churches have been the schools of democracy and the source of outstanding community care. Members of such gatherings are far more likely to be involved in voluntary community work than non-church goers. This should make us think hard about the philosophy of individualism compared to one of faith.

This experience of church community is precisely what modern culture is abandoning. We are increasingly being left with individualism on the one hand and, to fill the vacuum, the state on the other, as unions, clubs, lodges, voluntary associations, churches decay.

The issue is, will we, as a free people, voluntarily associate for good purposes, independent of the state? Is our individualism actually true freedom? I believe that individualism is just as great a danger to our true humanity as the collectivist spirit of Marxism proved to be.

Earlier I wrote of the liberal vision of society, in which we value tolerance, coolness, personal freedom, choice. Without doubt, the Christian view of society and the modern Western one have drifted apart. In the present world, talk of the kingdom of Jesus sounds divisive and even dangerous. It challenges the assumptions on which we build our lives: that I am my own master, that individual freedom is the greatest good, that if I wish to have fulfilment I will not yield myself to any Lord, human or divine. It seems to me that this is at the heart of the greatest issues facing us at the present time. Who am I? Who are we?

What does martyrdom teach us? Martyrdom does not demonstrate truth. There are martyrs for bad causes, as well as martyrs for good causes. The long roll of Christian martyrs may all have wasted their lives.

We can, however, say this: from the beginning, Jesus Christ inspired the witness of martyrs; their witness was of key significance for the triumph of faith in him in the Roman Empire. Unlike suicide-bombers, they did not die in order to attain life; they died because they had found life, in Jesus.

How? Because they were convinced that the death of Jesus was a demonstration of God's love for them, and that if he had died for them, they could die for him. It is no accident that the cross remains as the symbol of Christianity above all others. But if the cross of self-sacrifice does not touch your daily life, it is no good thinking that martyrdom will achieve anything. As the Bible puts it: "If I give away all I have, and if I deliver up my body to be burned, but have not love, I gain nothing" (1 Corinthians 13:3).

Dietrich Bonhoeffer, hanged by the Nazis for his part in the plot against Hitler, lived for Christ long before he was called on to die for him. He said, "When Christ calls a man, he bids him come and die".[8]

You would have to say that anyone who can inspire martyrs has a future, for the future of any movement will be carried by the sacrificial conviction of those who adhere to it. It will be one of the vital tests for the future of faith in Jesus that he can still find in large numbers those who will serve his cause at great personal cost, including, but only if absolutely necessary, martyrdom.

In this sense the spirit that makes the martyr for Christ is simply an extension of that which makes the ordinary believer: "If anyone would come after me, let him take up his cross daily and follow me" (Luke 9:23). Perhaps that is a clue to the future of Jesus. If men and women, not fanatics but people of conviction, are prepared to sacrifice for him, even to suffer for him, he has a future in our world. When there is no more such sacrifice, there will be no more Jesus.

5 | Jesus and the millennium— will he never come back?

Has God rejected Jesus?

According to Jesus, God's kingdom will come in two stages. The first arrived with him. The second is his return, in glory, to end all history and begin the new age.

To state the obvious, Jesus has been away a long time. Where is the promise of his coming? You may say, "Even if the kingdom of *Jesus* has entered the world, his continued absence shows that it is not the kingdom of *God*". As though Jesus is not endorsed by God.

One answer, accepted by many today, is that if we read history properly, we would see that God is at work, and that the imminent return of Jesus is quite likely. There are signs that point that way. Although talk of signs in history may sound 'fundamentalist' and culturally marginal, such ideas are widespread and to be examined seriously.

The greatest sign, many believe, of the return of Jesus is the emergence of Israel as a nation in 1948, followed by the occupation of Jerusalem in 1967. For millions of people, especially in the United States, these events were predicted in prophecy as a signal of his return. It's easy to be pro-Israel, if you see the very existence of Israel as part of God's plan for the world. This belief contributes to the political shape of our world, notably in the Middle East.

Here's an Australian version of this very widely held belief. In 2004, the ABC ran a competition to discover Australia's one hundred favourite books. Patrick White did not make the list, but Col Stringer did. Mr Stringer describes himself as 'Pastor Crocodile Dundee'. His book, *800 Horsemen,* ranked number 14. Mr Stringer says:

> When Jesus Christ comes back to the earth His feet will touch down on the Mount of Olives … One of the first sights to greet him will be an emu-plumed Australian slouched hat! Many Australians have no idea that over 200 Light Horsemen are buried in Jerusalem … overlooking the Mount of Olives, the very spot to which Jesus will return![1]

Col Stringer believes that nations have callings and it was the calling of Australia to contribute to the liberation of Jerusalem. Basically, his argument is, as you treat Israel so God will treat you. As a result, Australia will be blessed as a nation.

This whole idea may sound ludicrous to you. But before you pass by on the other side of the road, pause a moment. What do you think it sounds like to Islam? What does it say about Christian American support for Israel?

Let's look at things from an Islamic point of view.

One way to understand world events is to say that the West is a Christian civilization. Nearly a thousand years ago, Christians tried to wrest Jerusalem from Muslim control by force in the name of Christ. Now Christians support the State of Israel, which has taken control of Jerusalem. They are motivated in part by the belief that the return of Jesus Christ is at hand.

Islamic understanding is not the whole truth, but there is some truth in it. Many Americans believe that America is a special nation, and that part of its peculiar calling is to protect and support Israel. Under the mantle of this belief are forces that hope to influence the foreign policy of the last great superpower in the most dangerous part of the world.

In the judgement of historian Professor Emeritus Paul Boyer, of the University of Wisconsin at Madison, an expert observer of prophetic movements, "To understand American attitudes toward the Jews and Israel, one must attend carefully to the nuances and subtexts of popular prophecy belief".[2]

A specialist in Middle East history, Professor Irvine Anderson, formerly of the University of Cincinnati, concludes that "an American cultural disposition to support Israel, based at least in part on the influence of the Christian Bible, will continue to be one of the factors in the dynamics of policy formulation".[3]

Is the prophetic movement popular? We ought to note the immense success of the apocalyptic publishing industry. For example the books of Hal Lindsey, author of *The Late Great Planet Earth*, have sold 35 million copies. Likewise Tim LaHayes' and Larry Jenkins' 'Left Behind' novels, which routinely make the *New York Times* bestseller list, have sales of over 62 million since 1995.

And is it credible? The prophetic movement—usually linked to a theology originating in the nineteenth century called 'dispensational premillennialism'—also has its genuinely impressive scholars and places of learning. To regard these beliefs as the work of a tiny group of illiterate and unsophisticated people would be ill-informed. If they are wrong they need refutation rather than mockery. Indeed mockery is precisely what reinforces fundamentalism, if fundamentalism is a helpful description of this phenomenon. It is because the modern secularist thinks that such beliefs are beneath contempt that they have failed to notice them, failed to understand them, failed to examine them in their own terms. It is part of the all-too-common blindness of the secular mind to matters of religion and theology.

'Fundamentalism' is not refuted by a sneer; if it needs refutation, it is refuted by theology.

What gives these convictions their power to persuade?

First, they appeal to the Bible and the words of Jesus. For many millions of people the Bible is still *the* authority. It came third in the ABC's competition! Col Stringer thinks his views are biblical; you cannot persuade him out of them by saying that the Bible is entirely wrong. You have to demonstrate, if you can, that he has not read it correctly.

Second, they help fill a spiritual vacuum. They seem to me to be a religious version of the 'clash of civilizations' discussion. We want to know where we are in the historical time line, and we invest our moment in history with enormous significance as a way of saying that we ourselves are significant. We long for secret knowledge about the future. We are flattered by the thought that our nation may have a calling and that we are living at exactly the right time for this to be manifest.

Third, they have demonstrable, empirical truth on their side—at least so it appears. The coming into existence of the State of Israel in 1948 and its subsequent history appears to vindicate the predictions of the Bible in a dramatic and irrefutable manner. It captures something that modern Christianity has lost: the sense that history matters; that Christianity is not merely about cups of tea and being nice to each other, but about the dynamic of history itself. It reminds us that there is a kingdom of God set loose in the world, and that you can expect the Bible and the newspaper to intersect.

Such beliefs are certainly not the whole explanation of American foreign policy in the Middle East. Professor Anderson is much closer in his careful judgement that they provide a 'cultural disposition' towards favouring Israel. (Please notice that I am not myself entering into the debate about support for Israel or otherwise.)

But to go back to the original question: Has God rejected Jesus? Secularists and even some Christians have been saying for a long time that the future return of Jesus is unbelievable. It is simply not going to happen. Whatever Jesus may have meant for the past, he is dead and buried, with no future. On the other hand, in the return of Israel, there would seem to be the proof that the secularists have been wrong all along and that the final vindication of Jesus is at hand.

But what do I think? In fact, I do think that this particular way of reading history is wrong because I think that it is based on an incorrect and novel reading of the Bible. Although I respect the views of the scholars in this movement, I think it seriously misreads the original evidence. Let me explain.

To consider the issue of the timing of Jesus' return: Jesus does two things here. *First*, he declares his own ignorance of any date. "No-one knows", he said, "not even the angels of heaven, nor the Son, but the Father only". "You must be ready", he said, "for the Son of Man is coming at an hour you do not expect" (Matthew 24:36, 44). As unexpected as a thief.

Second, Jesus gives out a list of what seem to be early warning signs of his appearance: "Nation will rise against nation, and kingdom against kingdom. There will be great earthquakes, and in various places famines and pestilences. And there will be terrors and great signs from heaven" (Luke 21:10-11).

I can understand why such signs have always fascinated. Signs provoke speculation and excitement, especially in times of disturbance, and reflect at least a sense of purpose in history, of events having meaning, of direction and the gift of hope. We lack a large and dramatic story to be part of; we miss something to feed the imagination and nourish the inner life. Nations also have callings, as Col Stringer might say to an Australia hungry for the significance that comes from being part of a story. But when you study the whole list it becomes clear that, mostly, the signs lack chronological significance. They refer to events that have always been with us.

Has there ever been a time without earthquakes, wars and rumours of wars? Even the more specific or historical signs could refer to several events. Indeed, the list could be applicable to any era; it is a list, as someone once said, to make Jesus' hearers reckon on the end, but not reckon up the end.

Biblical signs are not signs intended to chart apocalyptic chronology. They are signs that say, "Be ready all the time"; that there is only one large thing now left on God's timetable, namely the return of the Son.

Two thousand years have passed. In biblical terms, that is neither here nor there. God has shown himself to work slowly. It is not so much the length of time that is important as the nature of the time; it is not how long it may last, but what you are intended to do with it that matters; it is time for getting ready for the end by making the most of the present.

I realize that history has a direction, and will have its milestones. But the words of Jesus make me less given to interpret it and more prone simply to live it. My apocalyptic expectations stand at the ready but they are not fully engaged.

The present popular form of dispensational premillennialism is a novelty, a 19th-century creation. This reading of the Bible goes back on decisions about the way to read and interpret it that were made very early in the church's life.

The key to the issue is this: the dispensationalists insist on a literal and physical reading of the Old Testament prophets; I insist on a literal but therefore figurative reading of the prophets. I say 'figurative' because I think that the prophets themselves intended many of their predictions in a metaphorical, or figurative, sense. Certainly that is how Jesus and his disciples read them. "My kingdom is not of this world", Jesus said (John 18:36).

I say that this was a decision taken in principle when the Christian movement began. Remember that the original Christians decided that they were not a sect within Judaism, but they were going to include both Jews and non-Jews on an equal footing. In order to achieve that, however, Christians had to 'translate' the expectations of the law and the prophets, and apply them to Jesus.

Why does Christianity not have animal sacrifice, circumcision, kosher food, a Sabbath, a temple? These are laid down in the Bible. The Bible also provided a history and a vocabulary of salvation—words such as 'redemption' and stories like the exodus from Egypt. Christians, rightly or wrongly, took over all these concepts and understood them—'translated' them is the better expression—through Jesus. He was the true and final sacrifice; he was the high priest; he was the temple of the Lord—the meeting place of God and human beings; he is the redeemer, his death was an exodus; he is the true and eternal Son of David and so the king of Israel.

Under David and Solomon, Israel had an empire; the prophets said that under a coming king it would have an empire once more. The New Testament says that the kingdom of Christ, in which he rules over people in all nations, is that expected empire, a spiritual one.

I remember once being asked during a television debate, "What do you have against pelicans?" What the presenter actually wanted to know was whether I kept the Old Testament food laws, which forbid the eating of 'pelican' (the word used in the King James version of the Bible)! Her point was that if I did not keep the food laws, how could I quote verses from the Old Testament on sexual morality? Was I consistent?

This is a worrying question but not because the answer is difficult. It is a reminder of how little corporate memory remains of a standard Christian reading of the Bible. Decisions about how to read the Old Testament were worked out in principle 2000 years ago through the teaching and work of Jesus himself. The answer is that Christians distinguish between the moral and ceremonial laws of the Old Testament. We keep the first, abandoning the second. And, by the way, I would think that the old law favoured pelicans!*

When I am thinking about the return of Jesus and the future of Israel, I read the Bible the same way. If I am right, the move of Jewish people to Palestine is theologically neutral. It does not lead me to support or to deny the validity of the State of Israel; it does not push me to one side or the other of the present political argument. Nor, let me say, does it offer any support whatsoever to nationalistic readings of the New Testament. I do not believe that we can read anything about Australia or the United States, let alone Russia or the European Union, in its pages; and the concept of redeemer nations, national callings and lights on the hill is pernicious. Likewise, the kingdom of God is not the same thing as the church—a distinction that is sometimes forgotten by that venerable institution.

The kingdom of Jesus is a universal one; as a result, his church transcends national and other human boundaries. The follower of Jesus ought to be a citizen of the whole world, just as he or she is a citizen of a nation. Our concerns for justice and wellbeing should not stop with national or ethnic divisions.

That is my assessment of the evidence. What we think of as a lengthy delay is not caused by God 'disowning' Jesus. But it does test our capacity to live by faith in his promises. And promises are very powerful things.

* Or 'osprey' as modern translations give it.

How much is his promised return still worth? What use are his promises? I would say that they are a power for good. It is health-giving to live with long-term promises; provided, of course, that they are reliable. Let me illustrate.

In a recent address, Dr Michael Carr-Gregg, a distinguished adolescent psychologist, gave a startling picture of today's teenager. He talks about society's problems being reflected in the classroom and describes many students as "growing up in a psychological wasteland, without nurturing or support ... Every day of the week, 13-year-old children make decisions adults used to make for them ..."[4] Observing the current massive information overload and its absence of wisdom, he says, "Never before have young people been told so much and never before have they known so little". Under the impact of marketers they have become "greedy little adults".[5]

Dr Carr-Gregg reports:

In my capacity as the Agony Uncle for *Girlfriend* magazine, hundreds of 11- to 14-year-old girls write each month of the anguish they feel following the dissolution of their families. Their letters are awash with a mixture of apprehension and confusion about their future and the changing relationships that surround them.[6]

He observes:

In contrast to the young people of the Middle Ages who knew they had an immortal soul enclosed in the shell of a mortal body, [and were] surrounded daily by evidence of death and dying, [our children are] stripped of community, tradition, and shared meaning. Many of our young people are spiritual anorexics, empty selves that are fundamentally a disappointment. And nature abhors a vacuum, so they feel this urge to fill the void, soothed and made coherent by consumer products, celebrity vows, and never-ending quests for physical perfection.[7]

Dr Carr-Gregg is even prepared to liken the current situation to the abuse of children during the Industrial Revolution:

> The question is whether or not we are actually standing on the brink of yet another ghastly era for our young people, a period that will be qualitatively different but potentially as serious.[8]

A number of the senior educators I have spoken to are equally troubled. They talk of emptiness, of misery, of pain and suffering, of lives blighted to affect generations yet to come; of tens of thousands of people hurt by the spiritual failure of our society and the failure of the churches to communicate a word that will transform lives and bring healing on its wings.

Our older generations have lost the art of transmitting community, tradition and shared meaning, among the very things that we need to nourish the spirit.

In the United States, a Commission on Children at Risk, which included distinguished medical and scientific scholars, has recently issued a report. The Commission was alarmed by what it saw as the failing standards of mental health among children. The report argued that we are biologically 'hardwired' (to use its term) 'to connect'.

It said that for human beings to flourish we need "close connections to other people, and deep connections to moral and spiritual meaning". The Commission maintains that we are "hardwired for other people and for moral meaning and openness to the transcendent".[9]

Whether the biological claims of this Commission prove to be true or not, the conclusions fit with the observations of Dr Carr-Gregg and, indeed, with commonsense based on long human experienced.

This is where the promise of Jesus' return comes in. Christianity is a big-story religion. It goes from creation to new creation and beyond, and inserts human beings into that narrative. It is the very antithesis of what postmodernism has done in depriving us of our sense of continuity and history. Its promises, via tradition, provide meaning and bind us into community. Promises are faith-making words.

Let's think about time and promises for a moment.

We are all aware of being at the mercy of time. Our experience is like standing in a stream facing the current. Time rushes towards us, we live in a succession of instants; behind us, it freezes. The past cannot be changed. We cannot grasp time or stem its onward flow. But human beings are not totally at the mercy of time. We can move in and out of it—imagination and memory are two gifts for transcending time. We may leave its flow in our imagination, and peer into the future; or we may leave it, and remember the past.

Another gift for transcending time is language, especially in the form of promises. Promises arrive from the past, and always look to the future. That is their nature. They are attempts by feeble and time-bound human beings to create stability in a chaotic and unstable world.

When I make a promise, I am trying to guarantee that at least part of the future is going to be predictable, safe, stable.

"I will be there."
"I will post the letter."
"I will pay the money."
"I will never leave you."

Sometimes to make sure, very sure, we swear our promise in the form of an oath, binding us to future duties. We make treaties, covenants, agreements, all to create relationships within which we can know the future and act appropriately in the present.

"I will leave you my estate", for example, may be a promise with a long lead time. Depending on the person who has made the promise, you may well spend it in the present. You may use money a little more freely; you may cease to be anxious about your future.

What do you do with a promise? Depending on the person who issues it, you trust it or you are sceptical; you believe it or you doubt it; you have confidence in it or you wait and see. If you have faith in it, you live with assurance inside the time that it creates for you. It extends your grasp of the future. It creates a relationship between you and the person who has made the promise.

When a genuine promise meets real trust in that promise, it becomes very powerful. A sort of unity of persons is created. That is why marriages are based on promises, and that is why we should be careful to think about what we promise when we marry. Our homemade vows may convey far more or less than we intend.

Think of the opposite. Where a person is a liar, their promises cannot be trusted and relationships become impossible. That is why marriages are so vulnerable today —we do not feel the same moral conviction about keeping our promises; or, rather, we do not want to engage in the hypocrisy of making promises we will not keep. Indeed the capacity of language to convey meaning has come under suspicion.

Now think back to what Dr Carr-Gregg and the US Commission had to say about our need for community, tradition, meaning and the transcendent. When we find promises that may be trusted, we begin to create community and meaning. As we draw on the promises made in the past, we look into the future with hope and we understand the present. Time begins to have purpose in this unity of past, present and future.

Of course, in human terms, our faith is only as good as the person in whom we are trusting. Even the greatest cannot always keep their promises. And death is a reminder that even the firmest human community will be broken. That future event is certain. Our time is bounded by death. The stream that rushes towards us bears death in our direction, a day at a time. And death defeats promises—even the deepest human community, marriage, is only "until death us do part".

What do we make of death?

Jesus did not see death as merely the natural end of life. For him, it is both a physical and a moral catastrophe for human beings, since it begins with corruption and ends in judgement.

His promises invite us into a relationship with himself, one that will defeat death and judgement. John records these unforgettable words: "I am the resurrection and the life. Whoever believes in me, though he die, yet shall he live ..." (John 11:25). His words of hope about the future, including his promise to come again, are intended to provide for us that solid platform of hope in a world in which, humanly speaking, there is no hope.

The belief that history—the world's story—is actually progressing towards a determinate end has profound present consequences, especially when that end is thought to be a righteous one. The existence of what I have called long-term, transcendent promises encourages us to create history, to fill the passage of time with significance. What we can see by trusting in a promise is not the meaningless static of accidental existence but the ordered unfolding of the world's story, pointing to a just End. And if you count suffering in opposition to that, you need to reckon with the suffering and resurrection of Jesus.

Far from being an opiate, his promises fill the present

with hope, and thus with energy. Because the future fills the present with meaning and purpose, we give ourselves to the needs of others, even to the reshaping of society. The Christian hope has vast social consequences. Furthermore, remorseless time and its sorry consequences are relativised, tamed, by this hope: this present time is *not* all we have; this disease is *not* the finale for me; this setback, this failure is *not* an eternal one; this rejection is *not* the ultimate word over my life; these words, deeds and thoughts of mine will *not* be forgotten—they will be remembered one day when my life is open before the judge; but then, this judge I will meet is the one who died to save me.

In short, as far as Jesus is concerned, his future is certain as to fact, but unpredictable as to time; we are to be ready for it, but not obsessed by it. We are to live inside his promises, trusting them to create community and purpose.

I asked before: what do you do with a promise? The answer, of course, depends on the person making the promise. You either believe or disbelieve it. You then act accordingly. By making promises, Jesus puts us into a time frame. We look back to see what the promises were; we look forward to see them fulfilled; we act now in the light of what is yet to be. But, naturally, whether you do this depends on whether you judge that you can trust him.

6 | Jesus, freedom and the choices we make

What future does Jesus have among us? Are we going to get him back into the conversation about how we live our lives? He is an acknowledged master of how to live well. Rightly, his influence to this point has been massive and he does not belong to the churches, as such, but to us all.

I hope to start a debate about Jesus and encourage people to read the Gospels. We need to have some understanding of what he said and did in order to have him at the table. But I also have in mind the question of the interested agnostic: "How can Jesus enrich the lives of unbelievers?" This question is at the heart of what I am trying to achieve.

The future of Jesus, and his value for the unbeliever, is all about freedom: about our vision of freedom and about competing visions of freedom. If Jesus is to have a future in our civilization, it will be because we have accepted his view of what makes a free person.

Recently, Sydney businessman, now politician, Malcolm Turnbull said this:

> The old sort of regime of telling people how to live their lives, be you a government or a churchman, is running out of time. Australians want to be free. They want to have independence. They want to have choice ... Now there are some people who distrust human nature and believe that people won't make the right decisions and that others should make those decisions for them. We err on the side of respecting individual judgement and respecting individual choices.[1]

These classically liberal remarks raise basic issues: "Australians want to be free ... they want to have choice".

Mr Turnbull sees with great clarity that freedom involves a discussion of human nature. To him, it is people who distrust human nature who want to restrict freedom. He accuses them of not trusting people to make the right choice.

But that's not quite right.

Is not the real issue: can we trust each other to use our freedom well? Will my freedom to bargain be at the expense of your freedom to look after your family? Will my freedom to open my shopping mall on weekends be at the expense of your freedom to have a weekend off form work at the same time as the rest of your family? The classic liberal account of this—that I should not harm others in the exercise of my liberty—is far too shallow to help in real life. Freedom of choice is no absolute. Our freedom is curtailed by our responsibilities; it is curtailed by what is morally good; it is curtailed by our circumstances.

No, that's not right either. Responsibilities, goodness and circumstances do not curtail freedom; they are the conditions under which freedom operates, the tracks along which freedom runs.

What if we made freedom the supreme human aspiration? Is it really true that human nature is so good that we can sum up our national ambitions by saying, "Australians want to be free. They want to have independence. They want to have choice"? Couple that, say, with an addiction to intense consumerism and what freedom do we have? And what freedom do we give to others as we make our choices? Is it relevant to observe that the more 'independent' we want to become, the more dependent we are as a nation on social welfare?

Freedom is not individualism. There is a deep connection between freedom, self-discipline and goodness. If you want a free society, you must attend to its moral health.

Mr Turnbull's version of freedom is individualistic, as though we live in a world where others have no primacy. It treats choice as equivalent to freedom, as though the mere capacity for choice brings liberty. It is unrealistic, being based on the idea that human nature is good and that we will therefore make choices which are good for ourselves and others.

I think that Jesus would dispute all Malcolm Turnbull's positions.

I *do* think that a strong measure of human liberty of action and speech is a real possibility in a moral society, where good is honoured and where love is the rule. Indeed, one of the reasons why we enjoy as much freedom as we do in our society is our historical commitment to just such a moral existence.

But what is the source of this moral health? What if it is to be the sort of humanistic secularism apparently embraced by the authors of the book I referred to in the first chapter, *Imagining Australia*? They seem to think that secularism will act as the neutral umpire for the rest of us. They seem to think that its values are the universal ones on which we can all agree. They seem to think that secularism is religiously neutral. They seem to think that we will find sufficient inspiration in such stories as Eureka and Gallipoli to want to embrace these values. They seem to think that Australia is inalienably and by foundation a secularist society. And they seem to confuse the rightful secularism of our system of government with the idea of a secular community.

I would put it sharply this way: because they are not aware of the significance in the past of Jesus in this country, they cannot give him a future. They speak of the nation's "commitment to a form of Australian humanism ..." where mateship has to be understood via "the humanist ideals of 'brotherhood', 'fraternity', 'community', and even 'love'".[2]

I have to say that where their book offers values, they seem either thin or to come basically, yet unwittingly, straight from Jesus.

After all, why are brotherhood, fraternity, community and love suddenly *humanist* ideals? They sound rather familiar to me as a Christian. Indeed, according to historian Henry Reynolds, it was the biblical notion that we are all brothers that helped preserve Aboriginal lives in the 19th century. Some settlers thought of Aborigines as belonging to a different species. Professor Reynolds quotes the missionary and protector of Aborigines George Augustus Robinson: "... they are my brethren by creation. God has made of one blood all the nations of the people, and I am not ashamed to call them brothers."[3]

My problem is such that values, divorced from the kingdom-of-Jesus story that made them live and made them valuable, will not survive. That story does not assume that humans are good, but it does insist that they are precious, and it demonstrates this by a love which involved a kingdom inaugurated by a crucifixion. That story calls on us to find our freedom in the discipline of self and love for others, not in the infinite expansion of choice and the infinite expansion of wealth.

Clive Hamilton, the executive director of The Australia Institute, said all this in his brilliant 2003 speech entitled 'Can Porn Set Us Free?' Mr Hamilton laments the way in which the promise of the liberation movements of the 1960s "did not create a society of free individuals"; he observes that we are "richer and freer than human beings have ever been, but—and there is the contradiction—we are no happier". As he points out, liberation has paved the way for the terrible addictions of materialism and pornography. This is exactly in line with what Jesus taught.[4]

Are we are a secular nation? One answer is that we are, thank God. There is nothing whatsoever in our laws to force people to believe in or to establish a particular church or religion. In that sense we have been secular virtually since the beginning. No religion, including Christianity, is privileged. As our Federal Constitution says:

> The Commonwealth shall not make any law for establishing any religion, or for imposing any religious observance, or for prohibiting the free exercise of any religion, and no religious test shall be required as a qualification for any office or public trust under the Commonwealth.

I am delighted by those words. They were added to protect us; they best suit the sort of society in which I would like to live; and I believe that they will actually help the Christian faith flourish best because establishment is the bane of any religion. I want freedom for religion or non-religion, yours as well as mine.

But that is not the same thing as enforcing freedom *from* religion. Mind you, a Constitution which also begins "Humbly relying on the Blessing of Almighty God ..." is surely not trying to create a nation in which religion is intentionally marginalized and rendered linguistically and publicly invisible.

Are we a secular nation? I have to say that we are not, and never have been, a nation of secularists. Of course, from the very beginning, before and after European settlement, men and women of various faiths, and none, were present. But the point I am making is this: there is a contemporary blindness to the presence and impact of faith, and especially the Christian faith, which has always been the most prominent. It is assumed not to matter.[5]

I have been arguing that freedom is a fine thing, but that it is not to be confused with individualism and the multiplicity of choice. In my account of freedom, it can be experienced by the very poor person, by the bedridden person, by the mother of five little ones, and even by the prisoner. In my account, Nelson Mandela was free in detention, and so was Aussie war hero 'Weary' Dunlop.

There is a freedom of spirit that comes from the sound desire to choose the good, and to serve others; indeed there is a freedom which is the gift of being mutually dependent that is far superior to the liberal view of ever-expanding choice.

True freedom can only be found in a moral society. Furthermore, a moral society can only arise when we understand the truth about human nature—that it contains evil as well as good. And I would say that we have a far better chance of constructing a more moral society in the soil of Jesus and his kingdom than in Eureka or even Gallipoli.

This brings me back to the future of Jesus and the nature of human freedom, remembering the startling claim attributed to him: "So if the Son sets you free, you will be free indeed" (John 8:36).

Mankind has 'come of age', we have reached the adulthood of the race.

Believe it or not, that's how we flattered ourselves in the 1960s, somewhere between the Holocaust and Pol Pot's regime, while murderous Mao was slaying his millions. It was immensely liberating.

We chose to invent the utopia of a secular kingdom of God in which all could have all their choices, and in which we would be free. In this utopia, which we now inhabit, we have never had less time or been so enslaved to work or addicted to shopping or so dependent on the government and on drugs.

Jesus had a different version of freedom based on a different estimate of the origin, nature and destiny of the human race, and of what constitutes the good life. He came preaching the kingdom of God and invited entry as being in our best interest: "Take my yoke upon you, and learn from me, for I am gentle and lowly in heart, and you will find rest for your souls" (Matthew 11:29). Dependence on Jesus promises strength, forgiveness and hope, even in the face of adversity and death.

That is what he said: become yoked to me; follow me; obey my commands; become my disciple. Furthermore, in becoming yoked to Jesus, we become committed to others. We are intended to practise freedom from the obsessive concern about ourselves and so develop a freedom to love others. Our central dependency upon him begins to liberate us from the false dependencies that enslave us.

We do not even need to hate ourselves as so many do. Jesus promises freedom from the adverse judgement we deserve, and freedom from the death that is our fate. This is an alternative version of freedom, in which freedom is found in commitment, in love, in service—because this fits best with the sort of relational creatures that we are essentially. In this version of freedom, you can be free in a prison cell; you can be free as a disabled person; you can be free even as a rich person.

There is no solitary Christianity, no lonely spirituality, no cultivation of the self for its own sake. The powerful Christian love ethic, inspired by the love that Jesus had for us, sets our face towards others: towards our fellow Christians; towards our families; towards our fellow human beings; towards our society.

Judith Brett quotes the marvellous slogan of those, both liberal and labour, who fought together in the 1890s against the exploitation of the workers: "the union of all who love, in the service of all who suffer".[6]

The Spirit of Jesus is in that. "… and where the Spirit of the Lord is, there is freedom" (2 Corinthians 3:17). But in the age of autonomy it makes little sense. Take Jesus' ethic too seriously and you will find that your time is no longer your own; that your money is no longer your own; that your skills are no longer your own; that your life is no longer your own.

The problem is this: what is human freedom? The kingdom to which our culture has consigned us is truly a kingdom of nothingness. We are free to write our own stories on life's empty page, to be the master of our own fate, the captain of our own soul. But do we have the moral and spiritual capacity to be so independent—or is it a new form of slavery?

The culture of autonomy has distorted our communications. We are now taught that no 'text' belongs to its author. Some would even go as far as to say that 'the reader is the author'. That is, interpretation is everything and no author has the right to insist on his or her own interpretation of a text. I believe that at the heart of this lies the determination not to be ruled by another person, not even an author, and certainly not God, the Author of all. We must suspect all texts; 'molest the text, lest the text molest you' as some of our senior high school students of English have been told. Where we wish to avoid a final external authority, there is every reason why we should invent our own language, our own reality.

Our own reality—now that's a lonely prison cell.

We mostly believe that human beings are innately good. Jesus without doubt thought that human beings were innately valuable; however, he did not think that we were morally good. If we have come of age, it is interesting to see that the old immature failings are still with us.

According to economics writer Ross Gittins, our shared family time at weekends is in danger. There are various reasons for this: the productivity of factories that can be kept open longer; the two-income family; the idea of choice in the business of shopping. But Gittins also calls it "an unintended consequence of our intensifying materialism".

He goes on:

> We need the shops to be open—and other people to be working—all weekend because of the rise of shopping as a leisure activity ... our increasing tendency to *buy* our entertainment rather than make it ourselves with family and friends.

At first, Gittins observes, this will make us a two-class society, in which the upper class rests while the lower class works; but this will not last. "By then we'll have reached the materialist nirvana: we'll be living to work rather than working to live".[7]

This is the description of a sad ... society? I am not sure what word to use. I don't think that love for your neighbour is the phrase that comes instantly to mind. Perhaps 'selfish', 'greedy', 'anti-social', 'sad', 'unloving', 'unloved' are more accurate.

I disagree with Clive Hamilton at this point. Strangely, he calls 'noble' the 1960s demand for "freedom from the fetters of career and family". Strangely, because most of us want career and family, and are sad to be without them.

We were actually created to enjoy work and love. Utopianism always founders on the reality of human nature. The utopia may be noble, but we do not have noble people ready to inhabit it.

This is one of my chief difficulties with the call for voluntary euthanasia. I remember the emotions associated with the lingering death of my mother many years ago. Our love for her was so powerful; her love for life was so powerful. But I know that a word, even a hint from one of us, that she was being a burden, would have seen her ask to go early. It would have looked like voluntary euthanasia, but it would have been something far more sinister.

And do you not feel that, even when it is someone we love dearly, we cannot help thinking about what a difference there would be for us—even financially—when that person is no longer there? Perhaps you are too noble for such thoughts to arise. I tell you that I am not, and therefore I am not noble enough to be involved in making such decisions. Money is not the root of all evils; it is the *love* of money that is, and I know the stirrings of greed. Perhaps you do too.

One of Jesus' great failures was with a rich young man. Forced to choose between his riches and following Jesus, he went away, sorrowful. To the surprise of those who assumed, as we do, that wealth and spirituality comfortably coexist, Jesus said, "It is easier for a camel to go through the eye of a needle than for a rich person to enter the kingdom of God" (Mark 10:25).

The chains that bind us are forged within ourselves.

Human beings were not designed to be loners. We were not designed to read the world for ourselves; we were designed to be loved, and to love. We were designed, that is to say, to yoke ourselves to others. We were designed to find our true adulthood in service. We were designed to have hope, to be fed with promises of a better time to be.

Jesus failed with the rich young man. But he succeeded with a rather unpopular man named Zacchaeus (Luke 19:2-10), also a lover of money, obtained by exploiting poor people. His spiritual addiction was dealt with: he was set free; he returned his tainted wealth, and became generous with his money. He illustrates what Jesus offers: forgiveness in failure; a transformed life; a reordering of our unruly wills and passions; a love that blossoms because it is the recipient of love; a word of promise that creates trust. That is how he enriches lives, families, societies.

I am asked: how can Jesus enrich the life of an unbeliever? My answer is: by setting a new and different and better version of freedom and adulthood before us. Not the maturity of the immature, where the key to life is independence of others, but the maturity of the one who, like Jesus himself, is willing to make binding promises and to keep them at all costs. And the willingness on the other side to trust in promises and so enjoy relationships.

And what if all should let me down? All should fail their promises? That is where, for your part, you must decide whether Jesus has failed or whether he continues to keep his word. Can *he* be trusted?

In these pages I have not said explicitly anything about how we are to relate to Jesus and God. But the idea of trusting Jesus raises that very issue. Faith in God is one thing; faith in Jesus unless he is God, is another.

It must be evident that if Jesus announced the kingdom of God and then initiated his own kingdom, he cannot have thought of himself as a mere prophet. The very claim he makes upon our lives, together with his promises to be with us, would be utterly inappropriate from one who regards himself as simply one of us. That he *is* one of us is clear; that he unites God and man in his own person is a necessary implication of what he did and what he said. Is it so in fact? Certainly when men and women have related to him by faith, they have done so on the basis that to turn to him is to encounter God himself.

There is a story which witnesses to this experience perfectly. It is said that Charles Lamb, the 19th-century essayist, was once involved in a discussion comparing the relative merits of Jesus and Shakespeare. "If Shakespeare were to come into this room, we would all rise to meet him", he said. "If Jesus Christ were to come in, we would all kneel at his feet." That is the voice of trust in Jesus: trust that he actually chose to enter the world to save us, and that we meet God in him.

Will Jesus survive? What is his future? Well, I can see his kingdom making great progress in some parts of the world. But here? His future may be threatened in a culture that values individualism so highly. Even the revival of spirituality is shaped by individualism. A culture of powerful materialism makes Christianity unattractive.

But there *are* signs of change, signs of dissatisfaction. Signs that we want to restore the primacy of love, and words that mean what they say. Then perhaps we will begin to value once more free associations of free men and women, who meet to encourage faith, hope and love, meaning, purpose and belonging; who join together to make this a better world because that is what God wants and for that end he has given us a pattern of what a better world may look like.

I know that there are many different reasons why we may not be interested in Jesus. You may regard the whole story as intellectually disreputable, for example; you may have been deeply wronged by the Church; you may have suffered, and cannot reconcile your suffering and the picture of a God of love. But in choosing the question of freedom, I judge that I have chosen the deepest issue of all, the point at which we either feel that Jesus was wrong—a mere failed prophet of the end times—or that he was right, and that his kingdom is where you belong.

I will come absolutely clean. I am not really worried about the future of Jesus without the Western world to support him; he will survive and prosper. But I am deeply concerned about the future of the West without Jesus.

He does not account for all we are by any means, but he accounts for a lot of what we are. In losing touch with him I fear that we will not have the cultural resources to develop spiritual health and a vision of the good life and the enjoyment of true freedom. I fear that we will not be able to give our children community, meaning, purpose and a sense of the transcendent.

The future of Jesus' kingdom in the West, then, depends on the willingness of a sufficient number of its citizens to respond to his confronting and promising word. And his fundamental word to us is about him, and about you, and about your freedom: "Come to me, all who labour and are heavy laden, and I will give you rest. Take my yoke upon you, and learn from me, for I am gentle and lowly in heart, and you will find rest for your souls. For my yoke is easy, and my burden is light" (Matthew 11:28-30). According to Jesus, responding will cost you all things; according to Jesus, it will give you all things.

7 | Jesus and the question of faith

Faith in general

Any reader of this book who has some academic knowledge of the debate about Jesus will recognize how frequently I have passed over matters of great importance. The origin of this material in a series of radio lectures partly explains this. I have certainly tried to give a presentation in which Christians of other traditions than my own could recognize something of Jesus. I could only put things in my own way, but I hope that it was not too much of my own way.

One subject which readers may have expected me to say more about is 'faith'. It is, after all, the crucial point, especially for those people who ask how Jesus could enrich the lives of unbelievers. Even though they seem to be sympathetic to the enterprise of talking about Jesus, there is still a sense that there is an unbridgeable chasm between them and the Jesus that I have described. There is a feeling that faith is easy enough for me (after all I am a professionally religious person) but hard for other people to acquire. Some have even said to me, "I wish I had your faith", as though the whole process of acquiring faith is a deep mystery. Others clearly feel that you can have either faith or reason, but not both. As modern people it simply seems more difficult to make 'the leap of faith' required to enter the kingdom of God.

These issues are vital. Indeed, Jesus himself made faith a big concern. After all, his key message was "… the kingdom of God is at hand; repent and believe in the gospel" (Mark 1:15). As I will explain, for Jesus 'repent' and 'believe' were really two sides of faith. Just to read the Gospels is to see that Jesus expected faith, and that it was by faith that people attached themselves to him. Sometimes he used that word itself, sometimes other expressions, but faith is the crucial requirement.

For example, when he had helped a very needy woman who was conscious of her own many failures, he said to her:

> "Your sins are forgiven." Then those who were at table with him began to say among themselves, "Who is this, who even forgives sins?" And he said to the woman, "Your faith has saved you; go in peace". (Luke 7:48-50)

Such a saying fits in with the emphasis of the whole New Testament that it is faith in particular that relates us to God, even more than, say, love.

What is faith? How do you acquire it? Is it a choice between faith and reason? What do you get by it?

The beginning point for me is the whole notion of 'faith' in general. I have always been puzzled by people who say "I wish I had your faith", as though faith itself is hard to come by. Yet faith is one of the most common of human attributes. In fact, we could not function without it even for an hour. We constantly exert faith. It comes to us easily and spontaneously via experience. We have faith in objects (such as chairs and trees), faith in ideas (such as the idea that money is a useful means of exchange), faith in words (such as a promised appointment), faith in persons (such as in a friend).

In our society we often value scepticism, and with good reason. But a general mood of scepticism is miserable; a state of radical doubt would be untenable; indeed it would constitute a mental illness. If you did not have implicit faith in a million things for every one that you were sceptical about, you could not survive in this world.

Faith is so commonplace that we have many words for it. We speak of *belief* in a remedy, *trust* in a doctor, *confidence* in a bank, *reliance* on a friend, *dependence* on a family member, *assurance* about a promise, *persuasion* that something is going to happen. All such expressions contain the idea of faith. You might exert faith for just a moment, as when you cross the road at the lights, confident that the motorist is not going to move forward; you can exercise it for a lifetime, as when you marry someone and trust their promise to be faithful day in and day out for sixty years.

In itself faith is such an ordinary thing we hardly notice it. Only rarely, in special circumstances, would we think that we deserve praise for having faith. When we say to someone, "I have faith in you", it is more a statement about *them* than about us. We are saying that the other person is trustworthy. If there is some doubt about this, because of past behaviour, we are issuing a challenge to improve. The significance of our remark lies in the fact that faith is a powerful thing because it joins us together. If you have faith in me we have formed a sort of community. You can exploit my faith in you; I benefit from the way in which we can cooperate. Thus, although faith is not particularly praiseworthy, it is very powerful, because it enables you to tap into power which may help you in all sorts of ways. Faith unites, for good or for bad.

Take your relationship with a doctor. You are sick; so you visit the physician. You need very significant levels of faith in order to receive help. In our society you take for granted a high level of professional competence. You are trusting the university and hospital where this person has trained; you are trusting whatever board has accredited him or her; you are trusting the doctor to have remained up-to-date in knowledge; you are trusting that he or she will be in their rooms at the appointed time. More than that, you are trusting that the doctor will give you 'professional' advice—advice which is not prejudiced by financial considerations or by racial bias or any other irrelevant consideration. When you are given a prescription, you trust that it has been written out properly and fulfilled correctly by the pharmacist. You carry out all these operations by faith of which you are unconscious because it comes so naturally to you.

Please notice that, first, you do not congratulate yourself for having this faith. It is not meritorious, or even particularly clever. Second, notice how powerful this faith is. It has taken you to the right person, given you the right attitude and led to your health being restored. Your faith has saved you. It has united you to the person who can give you the assistance you need. Together you are powerful. Sometimes mere faith is so powerful that healing comes without actual medicine. The doctor could have given you a placebo. Your confidence in him or her is so great that you take it without question, and the mere fact that you have related to the doctor and followed his or her instructions has been sufficient. But there are limits. You could have immense faith in the doctor and the placebo, but it will not save you from a genuine organic disease.

What would scepticism have done for you? It too has a key role to play. Unremitting scepticism would have condemned you, for it would mean that you would trust no-one. But, on the other hand, there is no great virtue in thoughtless or irrational faith. Mere faith without thought is dangerous. You have gone to the trained doctor because you are sceptical of the powers of the local New Age healer to offer an effective cure. It may be that experience has led to that view, or you may simply be persuaded of the superiority of modern Western medicine because of its scientific basis. Doubt and scepticism play a vital part in guiding us in the practical affairs of everyday life. But it has to be doubt in the right place and in the right amount, just as it has to be faith in the right place and the right amount. Neither faith nor doubt are divorced from what we may call reason.

A glance at the dictionary will show that 'reason' is a word with many nuances. But if we think of it as the capacity for, and exercise of, judgement, based on sound logic and good evidence, it will be close enough to its use in common speech. Sometimes, as in mathematics, the emphasis will fall on logic; many times, however, the art of reasoning depends on experience. Thinking through the evidence, weighing it up, coming to a conclusion, testing it out—these are the activities of reason which, once again, we exercise on a moment-by-moment basis. Such an activity depends to a large extent on the object that we are reasoning about.

Our reasoning has to conform to the reality of the thing we are judging. It is no good insisting that a bird act like a jellyfish, or that a game of football conform to the rules of cricket. Mere logic, disconnected from reality, is not enough. On the other hand, we have come to realize more and more the truth (which the Bible is very clear about) that human reason is strongly affected by our language, our upbringing, our culture. The exercise of reason is a struggle for us, especially when it demands that we go against our usual way of thinking, and consider something new and fresh. The exercise of reason is a profoundly moral matter, involving, among other things, a love of the truth, a deep understanding of ourselves, and a willingness to be open-minded about others. In the contemporary world we have come to understand these limitations to reason with such clarity that we are in danger of acting as though there is no access for us to such things as truth and falsehood, right and wrong. This is as great a danger as the exaltation of human reason to a pre-eminence that it does not deserve.

Notice, then, the connection between faith and reason. They are not the same thing, but they need each other: reason needs faith, and faith needs reason. They are not in competition. Reason makes you confident that the scientifically trained doctor is best for you; but faith means that when you arrive in the surgery you do not spend time examining the doctor's credentials to make sure that they are not fraudulent. Even the knowledge that some 'doctors' have forged credentials does not lead you to that level of scepticism. Life would be utterly impossible without faith. And that is completely reasonable.

The same thing applies to the practice of science itself. It is not as though science is all reason with no faith. On the contrary. The typical inductive method of scientific research is conducted on the reasonable but unprovable belief in a present and future consistency in nature. Likewise, all scientific research is conducted in the context of a web of other research. Scientists assume that their colleagues are telling the truth and that they are using proper methods. Again and again, they rely on the research of others.

Sometimes, of course, they check the research. They always agree that scientific conclusions are open to revision. But in the normal course of events it is entirely reasonable for academic workers to rely on the conclusions of others without doing the work themselves. Scientists are among the greatest users of faith, and this is reasonable. That is one reason why science is so powerful. It proceeds by faith.

Faith and reason are indispensable allies in all the affairs of life. But they are not identical. Sometimes it is necessary and justified to have a faith that goes well beyond reason. If, for example, while driving in the bush I come to a dangerous river, I may take a calculated risk in passing through it. I am relying on my experience and judgement, but in the end I cannot know whether I am making a good choice until I have actually passed through. By trust in my experience—that is, by faith working with reason—I have forded the river. But there is a risk involved since even reason cannot see the future or be aware of all the relevant circumstances. There is a limit to reason in everyday life.

Sometimes our trust is misplaced. There are, it appears, many people who have faith in good luck charms. Others trust their astrological stars. Others have a misplaced confidence in their capacity to pick winners at the races. In such cases, faith and reason are indeed at loggerheads and rightly so. Faith is not a good thing in itself. The consequences of misplaced faith can be disastrous. The power of faith lies not in itself, but in its object, and if you pin your faith on the wrong object, little good can flow. Faith has got to ask, "Is this reasonable? Does it make sense as far as I can see?" Otherwise faith is merely superstition.

Indeed, superstition is a variety of faith. Considered inwardly, or subjectively, there is no difference. You cannot tell whether faith is good or bad by the feelings it gives you. Nor is faith good or bad in accordance with the quantity of it. A full and unwavering acceptance of nonsense is still superstition, despite its inward conviction. Nor is it easy, or perhaps even possible, to bolster or create faith by a mere act of will. It is not as though we conduct an inner scrutiny of ourselves and then say, "I will have faith, I will have faith …"

Faith generally comes spontaneously as we are persuaded by the object of faith that it makes sense to trust it or him or her. Our 'reasoning' has to fit the object, and for this we use logic and experience and even intuition. Think of how all these things are needed by a batsman before he hits a ball hurled at him with great speed; in backing himself to strike the ball, he trusts his bat not to break, he has confidence in the pitch, he is trusting his fortunes to the umpire, he believes that the bowler will not throw the ball at his head. All this trust, belief, confidence—all this faith—is reasonable and necessary. It may prove to be wrong, but it is based on sensible grounds, especially past experience. It is not just superstition.

Faith in Jesus

Now let us apply these ideas to faith in Jesus. There are a number of points to make.

First of all, faith in Jesus does not arise because a person is better than others, or more naturally religious. It arises from a study of Jesus, not a study of faith. The person who trusts Christ does so because he or she is persuaded by hearing or reading about him that Jesus makes sense of experience and may therefore be trusted. This study of Jesus uses human reason, but it must use reason *appropriate* to the object of the study. I do not think, for example, that a determined atheist could make an appropriate study of Jesus because he or she would have *inappropriately* rejected much of the evidence *a priori*. Any object has to be studied on its own terms if we are to understand it and relate to it reasonably. Mere prejudice is not a substitute for reason.

Second, it is not the *amount* of faith in Jesus that is important, but the object of our faith, Jesus himself. Jesus talked about faith as small as a mustard seed being able to do great things (Luke 17:6). It is, of course, not the faith or even the amount of faith that accomplishes the great things; it is the one in whom we have our faith. That is why faith and doubt can, and for many of us do, co-exist. Faith takes us beyond reason because reason itself is so weak. But faith may still be misplaced; our judgement may well be faulty. Faith does not answer all questions, and it may well be tested, refined, even refuted by further facts or logic. All this is essential to the nature of faith, and hence faith and doubt are often found together. But the power of faith is not in the size of our faith; it is in the power of the person in whom we have our confidence. Small faith in a competent surgeon can lead to just as good a cure as full faith in the same surgeon.

Third, faith in Jesus may be mere superstition and hence useless or dangerous. The only way to avoid this is by the proper exercise of reason, discrimination, experience and common sense. There is an indispensable intellectual element in faith; it is not the opposite of reason, although it is not the same as reason. In my view, if we are assessing Jesus, it is relevant to have a sense of history, an awareness of the Old Testament teaching about the kingdom of God, an experience of human nature and a feeling for what makes morality. To lack these things is equivalent to assessing the works of Rembrandt without any thought or knowledge about either art or history. You lack the requisite tools to respond appropriately, and you would benefit from having someone with you who would help you see what you are in fact observing.

Fourth, faith in Jesus is not mere 'belief that' but 'trust in'. While there is an unavoidable intellectual element, there is also an unavoidable relational element because the object of your faith is a person. That is why in Jesus' teaching, repentance and faith are joined. Repentance is not mere sorrow over some failure; indeed, it is more than mere sorrow linked to a desire to change behaviour. When Jesus talked of repentance he was talking of the fundamental relationship between human beings and God. The invitation to repent is a summons to change your attitude to God and to put yourself under his rule or, to use the language of Jesus, to enter his kingdom. Faith in Jesus involves putting him in charge of your life, and completely depending on him in life and in death.

Fifth, faith in Jesus has a transforming effect. It receives what Jesus offers, namely a relationship with him based on forgiveness. Since it puts us in relationship with him, it commits us to obey him. The surgeon may cure you despite your faith; but it certainly follows that even the smallest faith will commit you to follow his instructions in after-care. Thus, for example, we are committed to keep Jesus' great command about love—to love our neighbour as ourselves. That is, faith in him, because it is faith *in him,* becomes the impetus for fruitful obedience to him. If it is a genuine trust in him, it will be the source of a life of service to God and service to others.

So where does all that leave me, as a 'person of faith'? Well, I completely repudiate the notion that faith is a personal, private matter, a matter of subjective choice divorced from reason. When in Western history 'Faith' was attacked in the name of 'Reason', both sceptics and believers had a tendency to make this response. Believers retreated to a burrow in which they could not be attacked because, they alleged, faith was beyond reason; unbelievers were content to leave them in the burrow where they could do no harm to anyone. If they chose to believe, it must be because they needed a psychological crutch. Allegedly, belief told you more about the psychology of the believer than about any state of affairs in the outside world.

As a result, even today, we have a communal sense that faith is private, both unjustifiable and irrefutable. I am struck by the number of media gatekeepers who seem to believe this. They express a respect for a position of faith, but cannot imagine that it can be held with any reference to the world of reason, of judgement, of evidence. And yet as exponents of the word they daily operate in a sphere in which human reason and human faith have to cooperate. It is hard to explain that what we need to bring to the discussion is a sense of what is *relevant* human reason to the assessment of Jesus, and also a sense of the *limitations* of human reason, including the prejudices to which all our reasoning is prone. For my part, of course, I must admit the possibility that if human reason is part of our response to Jesus, it may be that scepticism and unbelief have the better arguments. If I am ever persuaded of that, I would give up the faith and my ministry at once.

Christianity may be helpful or beautiful, but in the final analysis it must be true in order to command my loyalty.

And yet, I have to say that there is a sense in which faith is a gift. Otherwise we might make the mistake of taking pride in it as though it was an expression of our own goodness or our own cleverness. The danger would be that the God we believe in would then indeed be a figment of our own imagination. The whole Jesus story is nothing if it is not the extraordinary movement of God towards us. The struggle to be human, to make sense of the world, to be the sort of people we know that we ought to be, leaves us both helpless and undeserving of God's love. Hence coming to know Jesus is a matter of amazing 'grace'—a biblical word for love towards those who do not deserve it.

I have to say, using words that are inadequate for such a great mystery, that faith in Jesus has been drawn forth *from* me rather than having been under my control. And, given the sort of person I am, this is just as well. In the end, it is no more a decision to have faith than it is to fall irresistibly in love. Love is not contrary to reason; it incorporates and surpasses reason. Such love is both something that comes from you, and something which has been given to you. So, too, when I at last saw Jesus for who he is, I entrusted myself to him, for what else was I to do? I have never regretted this step of faith, for I have never regretted belonging to the kingdom of Jesus.

Endnotes

one

1. M Duncan et al., *Imagining Australia*, Allen & Unwin, Sydney, 2004, p. 32.
2. *ibid.*, p. 20. The 'fair go' is a traditional Australian colloquialism about justice and freedom of opportunity. To give someone a 'fair go' is to allow them the chance to do something without unfair conditions or interference.
3. Stuart Piggin, 'Australia's Christian Heritage: Taking Stock of our Spiritual Capital', Founders' Day Address, Christ Church Lavender Bay, 26 August 2005, p. 5.
4. B Dickey (ed.), *The Australian Dictionary of Evangelical Biography*, Sydney Evangelical History Association, Sydney, 1994, p. viii.
5. RW Emerson, *Nature and Selected Essays*, ed. L Ziff, Penguin, New York, 2003 (1982).
6. I have traced this quote, although in a different form, to HP Liddon's 1866 Bampton Lectures, *The Divinity of Our Lord and Saviour Jesus Christ*, Longmans, Green & Co., London, 1903, p. 150, which gives the details.
7. The Australian and New Zealand Army Corps (ANZAC) fought a famous campaign at Gallipoli beginning on 25 April 1915. Anzac Day, commemorated each year on that day, has become a potent symbol of national pride. The Eureka Stockade was a fairly small and short-lived rebellion by miners on Victoria's gold fields in 1854 over the cost of mining licences, taxation and other similar grievances.
8. Maureen Cleave, 'How does a Beatle Live? John Lennon lives like this', *London Evening Standard*, 4 March 1966.
9. Blaise Pascal, *Thoughts on Religion and Philosophy*, trans. Isaac Taylor, Simpkin, Marshall, Hamilton, Adams and Co., London, 1894, p. 142.
10. Thomas Carlyle, *On Heroes, Hero-worship, and the Heroic in History*, Lecture I, in *Sartor Resartus*, JM Dent and Sons Ltd, London, 1908, p. 249.
11. M Duncan et al., *op. cit.*
12. PW Barnett, 'Jesus, Paul and Peter and the Roman State', in Michael Nai-Chiu Poon (ed.), *Pilgrims and Citizens: Christian Social Engagement in East Asia Today*, ATF Press, Adelaide, 2006, pp. 63-77.

two

1. Ernest Renan, *The Life of Jesus*, Watts and Co., London, 1935, chapter XXVIII, p. 220.
2. *ibid.*, chapter X, p. 99.
3. *ibid.*, chapter XXV, p. 212.
4. *ibid.*, chapter XXVI, pp. 212, 215.
5. *ibid.*, chapter XVII, p. 149.
6. *ibid.*, chapter XVII, p. 150.
7. Albert Schweitzer, *The Quest of the Historical Jesus*, trans. W Montgomery, A&C Black Ltd, London, 1922, p. 1.
8. *ibid.*, p. 182.

three

1. Private communication from Dr Langtry, August 2005.
2. CFD Moule, *The Phenomenon of the New Testament*, SCM (Student Christian Movement), London, 1967, p. 3.
3. NT Wright, *The Resurrection of the Son of God*, SPCK, London, 2003.

four

1. Professor James Haire, '"Listening to the Voice of God": Building Communities of Peace for All', DT Niles Memorial Lecture, delivered at the 12th General Assembly of the Christian Conference of Asia, April 2005.
2. Paul Veyne (ed.), *A History of Private Life*, vol. I, Harvard University Press, Cambridge, 1987, pp. 208, 210.
3. Cited from J Stevenson (ed.), *A New Eusebius*, SPCK, London, 1965, p. 21.
4. Veyne, *op. cit.*, pp. 210-11.
5. Wayne A Meeks, *The First Urban Christians*, Yale University Press, New Haven, 1983, p. 192.
6. EA Judge, 'Did the Churches Compete with Cult Groups?' in JT Fitzgerald et al. (eds), *Early Christianity and Classical Culture*, Brill, Leiden, 2003, pp. 518, 520.
7. Rodney Stark, *The Rise of Christianity*, HarperCollins, San Francisco, 1997, p. 161.
8. Dietrich Bonhoeffer, *The Cost of Discipleship*, SCM, London, 1964, p. 7 (quoted by Bishop GKA Bell).

five

1. Col Stringer, *800 Horsemen*, Col Stringer Ministries, Robina, QLD, 1998, pp. 106-7.
2. Paul Boyer, *When Time Shall Be No More*, Harvard University Press, Cambridge, 1992, p. 224.
3. Irvine H Anderson, *Biblical Interpretation and Middle East Policy*, University Press of Florida, Gainesville, 2005, p. 4.
4. Michael Carr-Gregg, 2004 Wells Oration, Junior School Heads' Association of Australia, Melbourne, 2004.
5. *ibid.*
6. *ibid.*
7. *ibid.*
8. *ibid.*
9. Commission on Children at Risk, 'Hardwired to Connect: The New Scientific Case for Authoritative Communities', a report co-sponsored by the YMCA of the USA, Dartmouth Medical School, and the Institute for American Values, 2003: http://www.americanvalues.org/html/hardwired.html. Quotations from the Executive Summary.

six

1. 'Lateline', ABC Television, 19 August 2005. Malcolm Turnbull and Julia Gillard discuss industrial relations advertising funding.
2. M Duncan et al., *op. cit.*, pp. 30, 19.
3. Henry Reynolds, *This Whispering in our Hearts*, Allen & Unwin, Sydney, 1998, p. 23.
4. Clive Hamilton, 'Can Porn Set Us Free?', a speech given at the 2003 Sydney Writers' Festival: http://www.apo.org.au/linkboard/results.chtml?filename_num=15403.
5. There are exceptions. In Geoffrey Blainey's view, "Christianity in its heyday probably did more for Australia than any other single institution" (interview in *The Weekend Australian Magazine*, 29-30 January 2005, p. 10). Likewise, John Hirst begins his work *The Sentimental Nation: The Making of the Australian Commonwealth* with the bold words "God wanted Australia to be a nation" and goes on, as he must do if he is to be true to the evidence, to show how pivotal were religious ideas or sentiments to the making of our nation (John Hirst, *The Sentimental Nation*, Oxford University Press, Melbourne 2000, p. 4).
6. Judith Brett, *Australian Liberals and the Moral Middle Class*, Cambridge University Press, Cambridge, 2003, p. 21.
7. Ross Gittins, *Sydney Morning Herald*, 23 February 2005, p. 13.

Matthias Media is an independent Christian publishing company based in Sydney, Australia. To browse our online catalogue, access samples and free downloads, and find more information about our resources, visit our website:

www.matthiasmedia.com.au

How to buy our resources

1. Direct from us over the internet:
   – in the US: www.matthiasmedia.com
   – in Australia and the rest of the world: www.matthiasmedia.com.au

2. Direct from us by phone:
   – in the US: 1 866 407 4530
   – in Australia: 1800 814 360 (Sydney: 9663 1478)
   – international: +61-2-9663-1478

3. Through a range of outlets in various parts of the world. Visit **www.matthiasmedia.com.au/international.php** for details about recommended retailers in your part of the world, including www.thegoodbook.co.uk in the United Kingdom.

4. Trade enquiries can be addressed to:
   – in the US: sales@matthiasmedia.com
   – in the UK: sales@ivpbooks.com
   – in Australia and the rest of the world: sales@matthiasmedia.com.au